*A Life of Poetry*
*1948–1994*

# Yehuda Amichai
## A Life of Poetry
### 1948–1994

SELECTED AND TRANSLATED BY

## BENJAMIN AND BARBARA HARSHAV

HarperCollins*Publishers*

HarperCollins books may be purchased for educational,
business, or sales promotional use. For information please
write: Special Markets Department, HarperCollins Publishers,
Inc., 10 East 53rd  Street, New York, NY 10022.

FIRST EDITION

*Designed by Barbara DuPree Knowles*

LIBRARY OF CONGRESS CATALOGING-IN-PUBLICATION DATA
Amichai, Yehuda.
  [Poems. English]
  Yehuda Amichai: A Life of Poetry 1948–1994 / translated by
Benjamin and Barbara Harshav.—1st ed.
    p.   cm.
  Includes index.
  ISBN 0-06-019039-6
  1. Amichai, Yehuda—Translations into English.
I.  Harshav, Benjamin, 1928–      .   II. Harshav, Barbara,
1940–      .    III. Title.
PJ5054.A65A245   1994        94-7683
892.4'16—dc20

94 95 96 97 98 AC/HC 10 9 8 7 6 5 4 3 2 1

# *Contents*

## Poems *(1948–1962)*

## Now in the Din Before the Silence *(1963–1968)*

### Poems of Jerusalem

*Not to Remember (1971)*

## *Behind All That Hides a Great Happiness* (1974)

# Time (1978)

## *Great Calm: Questions and Answers (1980)*

## An Hour of Grace (1983)

## From Man You Came
## and to Man You Shall Return (1989)

### My Mother's Death and the Lost Battles for the Future of Her Children

## Even a Fist
## Once Was an Open Palm
## and Fingers (1989)

*To Hana*

# Now and
# In Other Days

✤✦✤✦ ✦✤✦✤

1956

In my childhood,
Grass and masts stood at the shore.
When I lay there,
They all rose above me to the skies,
I couldn't tell them apart.
My mother's words were with me
Like a sandwich wrapped in rustling paper.
And I didn't know when my father would return,
For, beyond the clearing in the forest, was another forest.

All things stretched out their hands.
A bull gored the sun.
At night the streetlight stroked
My cheeks with the walls.
The moon, a big jar, bent over
And watered my thirsty sleep.

My mother baked the whole world for me
In sweet cakes.
My beloved filled my window
With raisins of stars.
And my yearnings closed inside me
Like bubbles in a loaf of bread.
On the outside, I am smooth and quiet and brown.
The world loves me.
But my hair is sad as reeds in a drying swamp—
All the rare birds with beautiful plumage
Flee from me.

## ➤ BOTH TOGETHER ◄
## AND EACH APART

"Both together and each apart . . ."    —FROM A LEASE

My girl, another summer's gone dark,
My father didn't come to the Luna Park.
The swings are swinging. And we will start
Both together and each apart.

The horizon loses the ship's prow—
It's hard to hold onto anything now.
Behind the mountain, the warriors are set
For battle. We can use all the pity we can get.
Both together and each apart.

The moon is sawing the clouds above—
Come, let's start a duel of love.
Just the two of us will love before the hosts.
We may still change all evil ghosts.
Both together and each apart.

My love has made me, it is plain,
Like a salt sea in the first rain.
Slowly I am brought to you, I fall.
Take me. We have no angel at all.
Both together. And each apart.

# GOD TAKES PITY ON KINDERGARTEN CHILDREN

God takes pity on kindergarten children,
Less on schoolchildren.
On grownups, He won't take pity anymore.
He leaves them alone.
Sometime they have to crawl on all fours
In the blazing sand,
To get to the first aid station
Dripping blood.

Maybe He will take pity and cast His shadow
On those who truly love
As a tree on someone sleeping on the bench
On a boulevard.

Maybe we too will spend on them
The last coins of favor
Mother bequeathed us,
So their bliss will protect us
Now and in other days.

6      *Yehuda Amichai*

My father built a great worry around me like a dock
Once I left it before I was finished
And he remained with his great, empty worry.
And my mother—like a tree on the shore
Between her arms outstretched for me.

And in '31 my hands were merry and small
And in '41 they learned to use a rifle
And when I loved my first love
My thoughts were like a bunch of colored balloons
And the girl's white hand clutched them all
With a thin string—and then let them fly.

And in '51, the movement of my life
Was like the movement of many slaves rowing a ship,
And the face of my father like the lantern at the end of a parting train,
And my mother closed all the clouds in her brown closet.
And I climbed up my street,
And the twentieth century was the blood in my veins,
Blood that wanted to go out to many wars,
Through many openings.
It pounds on my head from inside
And moves in angry waves to my heart.

But now, in the spring of '52, I see
More birds have returned than left last winter.
And I return down the slope of the mountain
To my room where the woman's body is heavy
And full of time.

## ✦ UN HEADQUARTERS IN THE ✦
## HIGH COMMISSIONER'S
## RESIDENCE IN JERUSALEM

The mediators, reconcilers, compromisers, appeasers
Live in the white house,
And receive their food from far away,
Through sinuous channels, dark veins, like a fetus.

And their laughing secretaries with rouged lips,
And the burly drivers waiting downstairs, like horses in a stable,
And the shade trees with roots in no-man's-land,
And the illusions are children who go out to pick cyclamens in the field
And do not come back.
And the thoughts pass overhead, like reconnaissance planes,
And take photos and return and develop pictures
In sad dark rooms.

And I know they have heavy chandeliers,
And the child I was sits on them and swings
Back and forth, back and forth, back with no return.

And then comes night to draw
Rusty and crooked conclusions from our old lives,
And above all the houses, the melody gathers the scattered words
Like a hand gathering crumbs on a table
After the meal, as the conversation goes on
And the children fall asleep.
And the hopes come to me as brave sailors,
Discoverers of continents, come to an island,
And sit upon me for a day or two,
Resting . . .
Then sail off.

## ➤ I WAS WAITING FOR MY GIRL ➤
## AND HER STEPS WERE ABSENT

I was waiting for my girl and her steps were absent.
But I heard a shot.—Soldiers
Training for war.
Soldiers are always training for some war.

Then I opened my shirt collar
And the two tips of my lapels pointed
To one direction and to the other direction,
And my neck rose between them—and on it
The crest of my quiet head
With my eyes, the fruit.

And below, in my warm pocket, the clink of my keys
Gave me some security
Of all the things you can still
Lock and keep.

And my girl still walks in the streets,
Wearing the jewelry of the end
And the beads of the horrible danger
Around her neck.

# ✦ RAIN ON THE BATTLEFIELD ✦

*To the memory*
*of Dicky*

Rain falls on the faces of my friends.
My living friends, who
Cover their heads with a blanket—
And my dead friends, who
Don't.

10     *Yehuda Amichai*

# THE SMELL OF GASOLINE
## IN MY NOSE

The smell of gasoline in my nose,
In my palm I hold your soul that rose,
Like an *etrog* in a bowl of soft cotton—
My dead father did it every autumn.

The olive tree stopped wondering—it knows
There are seasons and it's time to go.
Wipe your face, my girl, stand by me for a while,
As in a family picture, show your smile.

I packed my shirt and my gloom,
I won't forget you, girl in my room,
My last window before the desert and the gore,
That has no windows and has a war.

Once you laughed, now there's silence in your eyes,
The beloved country never cries,
The wind will rustle in the rumpled bed—
When will we sleep again head to head?

In the earth, raw materials leave their mark,
Not extracted like us from silence and dark,
A jet makes peace in the sky for all,
For us, and all those who love in the fall.

And after all that—the rain.
When we learned to read the book of lingering
And the book of parting,
When our hair learned all the winds
And our sweet free hours
Are trained to run all around
In the ring of time.

After all that—the rain.
A big salty sea
Comes to us, stammering
Sweet and heavy drops.

And after all that—the rain.
See, we too
Pour down
To the one who receives us and doesn't remember,
The spring earth.

*from*
➤ SIX POEMS FOR TAMAR ➤

### 2

Your laughter likes grapes:
Lots of green, round laughs.

Your body full of lizards,
All love the sun.

Flowers sprouted in the field, grass on my cheeks.
Everything was possible.

### 3

Always, you lie
On my eyes.

Every day of our life together
Ecclesiastes erases a verse of his book.

We are the saving evidence in the terrible trial.
We shall acquit them all!

### 5

Your heart plays hide-and-seek
In your veins.

Your eyes still warm as beds,
Time lay in them.

Your thighs—two sweet yesterdays,
I am coming to you.

All hundred and fifty Psalms
Shout together.

Sometimes pus,
Sometimes poetry—

Always something secreted,
Always pain.

My father was a tree in the Fathers' Grove,
Covered with green mold.

Oh, widows of flesh, orphans of blood.
I must flee.

Eyes sharp like can openers
Opened heavy secrets.

But through the wound in my chest
God peeps at the world.

I am the door
In His abode.

My father, suddenly, left all the places
For his strange, distant spaces.

We went to call his God, to bow:
May God come and help us now.

And God takes pains, is coming soon,
He hung His coat on the hook of the moon.

But our father, who went out on this endeavor—
God will keep him there forever.

Your life and death, father,
Lie on my shoulders.
My little wife will bring
Us water.

Let us drink, father,
To the flowers, to the ideas,
I who was your hope
Now am hoped no more.

Your open mouth, father,
Sang and I didn't hear.
The tree in the yard was a prophet
And I didn't know.

Only your walk, father,
Still walking in my blood.
Once you were my guardian,
Now I am your guard.

# ✦ LOOK, THOUGHTS, AND DREAMS ✦

Look, thoughts, and dreams weave above us
Woof and warp, a camouflage net.
The reconnaissance planes and God
Will never know
What we really want,
Where our road leads.

Only the voice rising at the end of a question
Still rises above the words and hangs overhead,
Cannon shells tore it like a banner,
A tattered cloud.

Look, we too are going
Backward on the flower path:
Starting with a calyx rejoicing in the light,
Down with the stem growing serious,
Reaching the closed earth, waiting there a little,
And ending as a root, in the darkness, in the womb.

From all the spaces between times,
From all the gaps in the ranks of soldiers,
From the cracks in the wall,
From doors we didn't close tight,
From arms we didn't twine,
From the distance between body and body we didn't close—
Grows the big expanse,
The plain, the desert,
Where our soul will roam with no hope
When we die.

Pinecones on the tree above.
In the heart below, dreams of love.

Our shoes, gaping, on the side,
See the sky. The highway, wide,

Reached almost here—but thinking of
The bit of eternity that a lover and his love

Found here, close to their everyday drone,
Made a detour and left them alone.

———

If the Flood comes down again, we too
Will be taken in the Ark, two by two—

With Mr. and Mrs. Elephant, Mr. and Mrs. Mouse,
Every pure and impure and his spouse.

Noah will protect us, keep us curled
As a vine sapling for the good world.

———

Like two associations in one head:
If they mention me, you are also said.

Like two candles in a chandelier:
You alone or I alone, far or near,

Too dark to read a paper, good and deep,
Too light to fall asleep.

But burning together—it's a holiday of light,
Put out together—a black night.

———————

We are two stones, at the bottom of a slope.
We rolled down here. Now we can rest, I hope.

We'll lie here for a year or two at last,
Watching the summers and autumns go past.

Our bodies rough, all face, to sense
The sun, the clouds, their difference.

And underneath, even in summer days,
Damp springtime earth, spinning in a daze,

Teeming black life, yet not cracking apart—
It's only ours, unknown, just in our heart.

———————

We are two digits wondering whether
We shall be close, added together

Or subtracted, for in the end the sign
Changes too from time to time.

It was so hard until we reached the point
Where we could stand together, thus conjoint,

We knew the multiples of bliss, and fractions,
As digits would, with no undue distractions.

Now, underneath us, the world is a rift—
Don't be scared, but lift

Your eyes, see how beyond the line blooms straighter
The common denominator.

# ❧ NOW THAT THE WATER ❧
## PRESSES HARD

Now that the water presses hard
On the walls of the dam,
Now that the returning white storks
In the middle of the firmament
Turn into flocks of jet planes,
We will feel again how strong are the ribs,
How bold the warm air in the lungs,
How urgent the daring to love in the open plain,
When great dangers arch overhead,
And how much love is needed
To fill all the empty vessels
And the watches that stopped telling time,
And how much breath,
A blizzard of breath,
To sing the little Song of Spring.

## ✳ I TOLD YOU IT WOULD BE SO— ✴
## AND YOU DIDN'T BELIEVE

Near the train, we saw layers of rock in a row,
Arches on arches, an ancient mass.
We too shall be like that, perhaps tomorrow,
Embracing, together, and high above us—the grass.
I told you it would be so—and you didn't believe.

All night the moon madly worked its plow,
Calmed blood and water, blurred opposites, too.
My girl, there is no difference now,
What happens to the world will happen to the two.
I told you it would be so—and you didn't believe.

The stove and the pot do not care whether,
They murmur to one another, cajole and beseech.
We too shall be like that together,
Red and warm, whispering each to each.
I told you it would be so—and you didn't believe.

There is a melody in us, but not enough thunder.
When will we learn at last to be hard and sure?
The lions, my girl, they never know hunger,
Only saints and lambs are hungry and poor.
I told you it would be so—and you didn't believe.

See, now our love has no bounds,
We came to a frontier where there is no more love.
The gate is locked, the guards on their rounds.
The children went home, the light went out above.
I told you it would be so—and you didn't believe.

*from*
✦ HERE WE LOVED ✦


*Sonnet Cycle*


**1**

Four years my father fought their wars in vain,
He didn't hate or love his enemy.
And yet, I know, day after day, he'd strain
To build me there from his tranquillity

So rare, he'd gather it and put it back,
Between the bombs and smoke there all about,
Into his tattered military pack,
Along with crumbs of mother's cake, dried out.

And in his eyes he gathered nameless dead,
He gathered many dead for me, to know
Them in his eyes, and not to share their dread,

And not to die like them. His gaze was strong,
He filled his eyes with them . . . And he was wrong:
To all my wars it's I who have to go.


**2**

The thoughts came in to him—a convoy run
Of supply trucks before the battle's fought.
They clearly reached him one by one by one,
And he unloaded them and always thought

Them in grammatical, full sentences.
The shots were periods, commas. Shells would move
The earth in blasts, and he would dress
My image, calm, a coating on his love.

*A Life of Poetry*     23

In spring, as in fresh twigs, a feeling caught him
In his fingertips, like an itch of blossom
And he prepared for fruit . . . But in the autumn

He, wounded in both legs, embraced the awesome
Earth. And falling down, like Balaam, he saw
A vision: my whole life, and blessed in awe.


### 3

Lips of the dead naively whispered words
Inside the frozen earth, their spirits looming.
And all the trees filled up with migrant birds,
In terribly exaggerated blooming.

The bandages again ripped off by force,
The earth does not want healing, just wants pain.
The spring here has no calm and no remorse,
The spring is alien country here again.

With pairs of lovers we were sent ahead.
As an advance patrol, we went to spy
A land beyond the rainbow in the sky.

And then we knew, the dead are coming back,
And then we knew, the storm in its wild whirl
Emerges from the soft palm of a girl.


### 4

Doves sit on shoulder and on window sill,
Our heart alone deep inside, lit with grace.
But like the water pipes that burst to fill,
We filled up now as high as to our face.

Sometimes the earth itself does not refrain,
Sometimes they sprout, like secrets long held back:
The chirping, budding, longing love in rain,
The joy, the waving at a railroad track.

And from a deeper place, the plants unfurl
Like memories, the flowers in the field
Rise up above the ground and do not yield.

And on the face of our beloved girl
Red spots as of anemones and pain
Flush shyly, for heart's passion had its reign.

### 5

The birds return without a rhyme or reason.
New cars pass on the highway, run and breathe.
We know again the song that comes in season,
The dead bequeathed to us what we bequeath.

Again our feelings, budding in our brains,
Will learn to walk beyond the fence to see:
The watershed divides the winter rains
In strict directions between sea and sea.

And what has throbbed into our eager heart?
Our little inside, did it get its part?
The world wafts from our faces, you can tell.

At first it's ours still, its smell—our smell,
And then it flees, no sense and no regrets,
And then it is immense, and it forgets . . .

### 6

At night, as in a tomb, a pyramid,
Our room is sealed. And way above our head
A mount of silence, rising sand, amid
The generations standing at our bed.

And when our bodies sleep, the road is drawn
Upon the walls again, where our souls float.
Our souls are passing by and, see: they're gone.
You see? Two standing in a passing boat,

The rest are rowing. Stars above us climb.
And other people's stars, the stream of time
Bears them without deciphering their plight.

And we are mummified in shrouds of love.
After eternity, dawn like a dove,
A merry archaeologist—he has the light.

# Two Hopes
## Away

✦ ✦ ✦ ✦ ✦ ✦ ✦ ✦

1960

## ❧ GOD'S HAND IN THE WORLD ❧

### 1

God's hand in the world
Like my mother's hand in the innards
Of a slaughtered chicken
On Sabbath eve.
What does God see on the other side
Of the window when His hands
Are inside the world?
What does my mother see?

### 2

Pain is a grandfather:
Sired two generations
Of look-alike pains.
My hopes built white tenement houses
Far away from the crowded dwellings inside me.

My girl forgot her love on the sidewalk
Like bicycles. All night long outside in the dew.

Children write the history of my life
And the history of Jerusalem
With moon chalk on the road.
God's hand in the world.

Let's fall asleep. Far from people's
Need to build towers. The network
Of longitudes and latitudes
Will hold us. We shall not fall.

The window is square. The bed almost.
The bitter moon is always round.
We needed to know so much,
But who could?!

Did you lock the door?
Imagine, all the words in the dictionary!
And I have so little to say to you.
And what will the night say, or the curtain?

Shall I put my hand on your pulse?
The others went off far away, to conquer.
The others always widen the horizon,
And ours is narrow, from hand to head.

We always have to bargain and haggle:
For one quiet night, ask for a thousand.
Yesterday we suffered, learned our lesson,
Tonight we shall forget, till morning.

Let us fall asleep. In the dark corridor
The electric meter will go on
Keeping score, all night,
Always awake, and we shall not worry.

*God-Full-of-Mercy*, the prayer for the dead.
If God was not full of mercy,
Mercy would have been in the world,
Not just in Him.
I, who plucked the flowers in the hills
And looked down into all the valleys,
I, who brought corpses down from the hills,
Can tell you that the world is empty of mercy.

I, who was King of Salt at the seashore,
Who stood without a decision at my window,
Who counted the steps of angels,
Whose heart lifted weights of anguish
In the horrible contests.

I, who use only a small part
Of the words in the dictionary.

I, who must decipher riddles
I don't want to decipher,
Know that if not for the God-full-of-mercy
There would be mercy in the world,
Not just in Him.

# ✦ AND THIS IS YOUR GLORY ✦

"And this is your glory"   —FROM A LITURGICAL POEM FOR THE DAYS OF AWE

In my great silence and my small scream, I inspire
Mixed kinds. I was in water and I was in fire.
In Jerusalem and in Rome. I may get to Mecca, too.
But this time, God is hiding and Adam shouts Where are you.
And this is Your glory.

God lies on His back under the world. There,
Something's always breaking down, needs repair.
I wanted to see Him, but I keep
Seeing only the soles of His shoes, and I weep.
And this is His glory.

Even the trees went off to choose a king.
A thousand times I started my life wondering.
At the end of the street someone counts out flat:
That one and that one and that one and that.
And this is Your glory.

Like an ancient torso with no legs and no arms,
Our life is more beautiful, without heroic charms.
Remove my undershirt armor, yellow in the night,
I jousted with all the knights, till we switched off the light.
And this is my glory.

Put your mind at rest, your mind ran with me all the way,
Now it's tired, worthless, you might say.
I see you open the refrigerator, my girl,
Illuminated in the light of another world.
And this is my glory.
And this is His glory.
And this is Your glory.

## WHEN I RETURNED THEY
## TOLD ME THERE'S NO

When I returned, they told me there's no
House and no matter. And I have
To go back to my wars
Where my own private blood will be shed,
For I was one, now many, soon again one.

For the world's birthday
They brought new ideas
Wrapped in newspaper and blood,
And I came empty-handed.
I was penniless, now poor, soon destitute.

I'm the last on the list and short in the halls,
But tall in the accounts of spring and love.
I'm one of those who hope a middling hope,
My windows are open. I don't want to leave.
I was my father, now myself, soon my son.

I've gone very far, the war increased,
My thoughts grew weary
And heavy like the arms of Moses.
And there was no one to hold them up.
I was where-from, now here, soon where-to.

Out of three or four people in a room
One always stands at the window.
Has to see the evil among thorns
And the fires on the hill.
And how people who went out whole,
Are returned in the evening
Like small change to their homes.

Out of three or four people in a room
One always stands at the window.
His hair dark above his thoughts.
Words stand behind him.
Before him, voices straying without a kit bag,
Hearts without rations, prophecies without water,
And big stones returned
But left sealed like letters with no
Address and no receiver.

Not like a cypress,
Not all at once, not all of me,
But like grass, in a thousand shoots,
Wary and green,
To be hidden like lots of children in a game
And one seeker.
And not like the only man,
The son of Kish, many found him
And made him king.
But like rain in many spots
From many clouds, to shudder, to be drunk
By many mouths, to be breathed
Like air a whole year
And strewn like blossoms in the spring.

Not the sharp ringing,
Waking the doctor on duty,
But rapping, on many windows,
In side entrances,
With many jittery heartbeats.

Then, the quiet exit, like smoke
Without fanfare, a resigning minister,
Children tired of play,
A stone in its last somersaults
After a steep slope, where the plain
Of the great concession begins. From it,
Like accepted prayers,
Rises dust in a myriad of grains.

Half the people of the world
Love the other half,
Half the people
Hate the other half.
Is it because of those and because of those
That I have to wander endlessly and change
Like the rain in the water cycle,
And sleep amid rocks,
And be rough as olive trees,
And hear the moon bark at me,
And camouflage my love with worries,
And grow like the wavering grass between railway rails,
And dwell in the earth like a mole,
And live with roots not with branches,
And not touch my cheek to angels' cheeks,
And love in the first cave,
And marry my wife under a canopy
Of beams supporting the soil,
And act my own death, always
Till the last breath and the last
Words, without understanding,
And make flagpoles in my house above
And a shelter below. And depart on roads
Made only for return and pass through
All the horrible stations—
Cat, stick, fire, water, slaughterer,
From the kid to the angel of death?

Half the people love,
Half hate.
And where is my place between the two matching halves,
And through what crack will I see
The white buildings of my dreams,
And the barefoot runners in the sand
Or at least the waving kerchief
Of the girl, beside the ancient hill?

# ❊ I WANT TO DIE ❊
## IN MY OWN BED

All night the army came up from Gilgal
To get to the killing field, and that's all.
In the ground, warp and woof, lay the dead.
I want to die in my own bed.

Like slits in a tank, their eyes were uncanny,
I'm always the few and they are the many.
I must answer. They can interrogate my head.
But I want to die in my own bed.

The sun stood still in Gibeon. Forever so, it's willing
To illuminate those waging battle and killing.
I may not see my wife when her blood is shed,
But I want to die in my own bed.

Samson, his strength in his long black hair,
My hair they sheared off when they made me a hero
Perforce, and taught me to charge ahead.
I want to die in my own bed.

I saw you could live and furnish with grace
Even a lion's maw, if you've got no other place.
I don't even mind to die alone, to be dead,
But I want to die in my own bed.

Thirty-two times I went out of my life.
Each time the pain grows less for my mother,
Less for others,
More for me.

Thirty-two times I put on the world
And it still doesn't fit me.
It's too tight for me,
Not like a coat taking the shape of my body,
Comfortable,
That will wear out.

Thirty-two times I went over the account
And didn't find the mistake,
I began the story
And they didn't let me finish.

Thirty-two years I've carried my father's features
And dropped most of them on the way,
To ease my burden.
In my mouth, grass. I'm searching.
The mote in my eye I cannot remove
Began to blossom in the spring with trees.
And my deeds diminish
Evermore. But
Interpretations grew around them, as
When the Talmud grows difficult,
It shrinks on the page,
And Rashi and the commentaries
Close in on it from all sides.

Now, after thirty-two times,
I'm still a parable
With no chance of being a moral.
And I stand with no camouflage, in the enemy's eyes,

Old maps in my hand,
In the increasing resistance and between towers.
And alone, with no recommendations,
In the vast desert.

### 1

Like an old windmill,
Two hands always raised to scream to the sky
And two descending to make sandwiches.

Her eyes clean and polished
As on the eve of Passover.

At night, she puts all the letters
And the photographs next to each other,

To measure with them
The length of God's finger.

### 2

I want to walk in the deep
Wadis between her sobs.

I want to stand in the hot wind
Of her silence.

I want to lean
On the rough trunks of her pain.

### 3

She puts me,
As Hagar put Ishmael,
Under one of the bushes.

So she won't see me die in the war,
Under one of the bushes
In one of the wars.

*from*

➤ AT RIGHT ANGLES ◄
Hebrew Quatrains

**1**

In his prayer sands, my father saw traces of angels in heaven's gates.
He bequeathed me a road, but on many roads his son procrastinates.
Hence his face is bright. Mine is scorched, and abdicates.
Like a used office calendar, I'm covered with dates.

**2**

Once I knew answers. "Sit down!" said God. And didn't blink.
The wind now at rest. The world calm. I must, and I blow at the brink.
Trees sprout buds, not heeding me, if I flourish or shrink.
The world is covered with answers and flowers. I must think.

**3**

Sign of Gemini, star of luck, Capricorn, my star again.
Who will love the things that are naught and in vain?
I, who stand in the world like water in the rain,
I love the things that are naught and in vain.

**5**

Now I know where they live, like the night owls,
But I shall never feel my hands as a stranger's hand that growls.
God left me only consonants, took away all the vowels.
That's why my life's in a hurry. That's why my life howls.

**6**

I must think many stones till I have my true home.
I invent whole new seasons, till my hour will come.
I am writing long scrolls and don't have my signature yet. The earth
Will forget all the layers. Only my mother remembers my birth.

**7**

Streets have names, pains have names, ships have names on their prow.
Already spring. Already negotiations. But the document is signed by now.

My father wearing tefillin, and I am harnessed in dreams. I'm able.
The world is plowed in us, for them. For us, it is undecipherable.

## 10

All my words and deeds were lost between the writing and the reading.
Like the mound, my silence sprouts grass, a green bleeding.
As a hand to your ear, I put my body to my heart, for heeding.
But they're saying no more. I learned to listen, without interceding.

## 12

The most wandering thing is a heart that stopped wandering.
The thing most lost is a lost thing returned, wondering.
The most weeping mouth is a mouth that laughed between stone
And cypress trees, yesterday afternoon. It laughed alone.

## 14

On the cover of an ancient box, a parting man and woman are drawn.
On a dark mourning my life was inscribed like the flight of birds at dawn.
In a corner of destiny, as on a white kerchief, my name is embroidered, as
    minted.
On my face, many faces of others were printed.

## 15

Spring came. Different and quiet, anonymous blood in a spree.
But I saw girls, as light-haired and light-skinned as the sea.
Ants danced under the skies of my soles, I wanted to be.
But I don't know my sky, if to see or to sea.

## 16

Slowly, with the blossoms of understanding, I begin to grope
To compare my rainbow life to the life of a forefather. On his slope
He had a white heart of atonement and a beard as thick as a rope.
I am surrounded by his hopes as the Cape of All Hope.

## 24

Now my love explains me as the commentators in their prime.
Spring translates the world in all languages, for all time.
Our bread, a prophecy on the table. All words ring beautiful, as a chime.
But destiny works inside us overtime.

## 25

Great speakers hold their microphone to their mouths.
I, your head to my lips. Oh, lift my love to north and south
And all the winds. We have nothing to hide in our stammer.
We are simple, easy to learn, as words in an elementary grammar.

## 26

At the end of green spring, God begins
Like a smoking, terrible factory. Perhaps
To transform us like iron. Therefore, I shall put my profile
Between Him and the world: perhaps to link, certainly to distinguish.

## 28

Electrical strings are taut over all. The world is my oud.
I sing: lo and behold. My food gets cold. Nothing is lost for good.
No more excuses of doors and locks, all is destiny, written in stone.
The angel will descend. I am ready, stretched like an airfield, and alone.

## 29

The frogs of expectation leaped out of me and came back.
My water is shallow. The world is not bad. On track.
With Columbus's eye, I discover a flower in the daily hack.
With an engineer's hand, I draw my life in poetry, there and back.

## 30

I once fled, I don't recall from what God, for what wish.
Hence I travel in my life like Jonah inside his dark fish.
In the world's guts, my fish and I get along quite devilish:
I will not abandon him. He won't digest me as a dish.

## 31

I don't know what is good or bad for me hereabout.
They left me my life as a new appliance without
Instructions: with what utensil and by what route
Must I repair the bad, to make it good, full of clout.

## 32

Death was round and open as two halfs of an orange in sight.
Now it's autumn: clouds pasted like posters to the night.

We didn't flee: your hair was caught in my thought, my tight
Life in your veins. Your destiny packed in my knapsack. All is right.

### 33

Now it's autumn. All glasses broken at weddings, didn't bounce.
All records are broken, I cannot change it by an ounce.
After the first rain, after the dead, all invitations to renounce.
The wind always goes over us, as over accounts.

### 37

I live now inside an abandoned love, like a guest.
When did the tenants leave? Did they find what is best?
I discovered it at a hard time of unrest.
And I live in it now. So far, I have no request.

### 41

Dust covers all the things mentioned above.
Dust is God's weariness in the world, whereof
It covers my rifle, my mouth that answers, my mouth that asks,
The travels of my blood and the hands of the angel ending our tasks.

### 43

Two hopes away from the battlefield, I had a vision of peace.
My tired head must go, my feet dream a dream, do not cease.
The scorched man said: I'm the bush that burned with no trace.
You may. Leave your shoes on your feet. This is the place.

### 45

A young soldier lies in spring, cut off from his name.
His body sprouts and blossoms. The blood of every vein
Is small and ignorant, chattering with no rein.
God cooks the kid in its mother's pain.

### 47

In the end, we too will be winds from beyond the rim
Of window, of east, of hope. We shall be the glim
Of a beautiful horse power and flower power. We shall be the pseudonym
Of the world and of the other sea, where we didn't learn to swim.

# Poems

✴✴✴✴ ✦✦✦✦

## 1948–1962

As for the world,
Like the pupils of Socrates: I walk at its side,
Hear its seasons and origins,
And what is left for me to say is:
Yes, it is indeed so.
You're right again.
You do indeed make sense.

As for my life, I am always
Venice:
What others have as streets,
In me—flowing, dark love.

As for the scream, as for the silence,
I am always a *shofar*:
Gathering all year long the one blast
For the Days of Awe.

As for deeds,
I am always Cain:
Wandering around before the deed I shall not do,
Or after the deed
I cannot undo.

As for the palm of her hand,
As for the signs of my heart,
The designs of my flesh,
As for the writing on the wall,
I am always ignorant: I cannot
Read or write,
My head is like the heads of weeds,
Silly grasses who know just
Whispering and swaying in the wind,
When destiny passes through me
To some other place.

In the place where I never was
I never shall be.
The place where I was, as if
I never was there. Human beings wander away
Far from the place of their birth
And far from the words their own
Mouth uttered,
No more within the promises
That were promised.

And they eat standing up, and die sitting,
And remember lying.

And what I shall never return
To see, I must love for ever.
Only a stranger will return to my place. But I shall
Inscribe the things again, like Moses,
After breaking the first tablets.

## ✦ IN THE MIDDLE OF THIS CENTURY ✦

In the middle of this century we turned to each other
With half a face and full eyes
Like an ancient Egyptian painting,
For a short while.

I stroked your hair
Against the direction of the march.
We called each other
Like names of cities that one passes through
Along the road.

Beautiful is the world waking up for evil.
Beautiful is the world falling asleep for sin and grace.
In the discordance of our being together, you and I.
Beautiful is the world.

The earth drinks people and their loves
Like wine, in order to forget. Impossible.
Like the contours of the mountains of Yehuda,
We too will not find peace.

In the middle of this century we turned to each other,
I saw your body, casting a shadow, waiting for me.
The leather straps of a long voyage
Are tightened diagonally across my chest.

I spoke words in praise of your mortal loins,
You spoke words in praise of my transient face,
I stroked your hair in the direction of the march,
I touched the heralds of your end,
I touched your hand that never slept,
I touched your mouth that perhaps will sing.

The dust of the desert covered the table,
We did not eat on it.
But I wrote on it with my finger the letters of your name.

Fare thee well, it was your face, and now the face of memory.
The ghost of wandering is conjured up, and flies and flies.
The face of animals, of water, face of leaving.
Whispering forest, face of womb, of infant cries.

No more the hour we can approach each other,
"Now, now"—such words we cannot say at all.
Yours was the name of winds, once woman
Of directions, and intentions, mirror, Fall.

For what we did not understand, we sang together.
Of generations, of the dark, the face of change.
No more my own, for me no more deciphered,
Nipples, buckle, mouths, screws—all closed and strange.

Peace upon you, who never falls asleep,
All was done by our will, and all is sand.
From now on, you yourself beget
Your dreams: the world is in your hand.

Fare thee well, the packs, the valises of death.
The strings, the mess of living. The hair's last ember.
For what will no more be, no hand is writing.
And what was not of flesh, we won't remember.

# ❖ AND THE MIGRATION ❖
## OF MY PARENTS

And the migration of my parents
Has not subsided in me. My blood goes on sloshing
Between my ribs, long after the vessel has come to rest.
And the migration of my parents has not subsided in me.
Winds of long time over stones. Earth
Forgets the steps of those who trod her.
Terrible fate. Patches of a conversation after midnight.
Win and lose. Night recalls and day forgets.
My eyes looked long into a vast desert
And were calmed a bit. A woman. Rules of a game
I was not taught. Laws of pain and burden.
My heart barely ekes out the bread
Of its daily love. My parents in their migration.
On Mother Earth, I am always an orphan.
Too young to die, too old to play.
The weary hewer and the empty quarry in one body.
Archaeology of the future, repositories
Of what was not. And the migration of my parents
Has not subsided in me. From bitter nations I have learned
Bitter tongues for my silence
Among these houses, always like ships.
And my veins and my sinews, a thicket
Of ropes I cannot unravel. And then
My death and an end to the migration of my parents.

It will be cloudy. There will be rain.
We shall be and die. Be awake.
There will be dozing breezes. I will see
You in the first difficult excitement.
You will see me, like a rain falling
In your face lifted to me. It will be cold,
There will be highs, there will be lows. And to whom
Will we speak if we won't be anymore? There will be
Good conditions for lovers on the ancient mound.
From all four sides of my life, the wind will come. It will be dark.
There will be waves. It won't be moderate.
There will be a cloud. There will be a rainbow in your body.
We shall not be the day after. It will be cold
In the valleys. There will be fog. We shall scatter.

Bend your head outside the window,
Wires may be caught in your hair.
Confuse the schedule.
Understand me. Experience
Your last experience. Roll up your dress
And do not show the ticket
For inspection. Let no one know
Where you're going.
Throw a burning cigarette through the window.
Cause a conflagration outside,
Big sister of the conflagrations in my eyes.
Leave the door open.
Leave the earth open.
Throw. Lean on. Take out. Do not
Show your identity. Do not get up
Before the old. Sit on your return. Talk.
Love me.

It is sad to be
The mayor of Jerusalem.
It's terrible.
How can a human being be mayor of such a city?
What is he going to do with her?
He'll build and build and build.

At night, the stones of the mountains around her
Come close to the houses,
Like wolves, closing in to wail at the dogs
Who became slaves to human beings.

### 1

The smell of geranium
Makes my memory spin.
In you, my weariness
Found an inn.

Even oleander
Will not remain.
What was, will never
Return again.

Untying as an oath:
Your buckle, your dress.
What rustled in the room
Will not regress.

A fossilized leaf,
Of ages a mime,
On the window sill.
Let's fall into time.

All that covered us up.
In the long night,
Our tempest inside
Will also be light.

Shine of silk and knife,
The distant sea.
A chair that moved.
Cover you, cover me!

### 2

The hair dried last.
We were far from the sea.
Words and salt that mingled with us

Separated with a sigh.
The primeval signs in your body
Didn't show anymore.
In vain did we forget some things at the shore
As an excuse to return.
We didn't.

I remember those days,
Named after you like the name of a ship.
Through two open doors, we saw
A man thinking. We watched the clouds
With the ancient gaze inherited from our forefathers
Waiting for rain.
At night, when the world grew chill,
Your body kept its heat a long time,
Like the sea.


3

No, no, you said.
Through the window, the light played
Miracles on your body,
Greater than the miracles
That happened to me in the desert.

No, no, you said.
And you were beautiful like the wasted time.
And on the Ninth of Av, Jerusalem
Was burned before our eyes.

And a year later,
It was we who were burned
Before the eyes of the white city.


4

It was a summer, or its end. I heard
Your steps walking from east to west
For the last time. Kerchiefs, books, people
Were forgotten in the world.

It was a summer, or its end,
There were afternoon hours,
You were.
For the first time, you wore your shroud
And didn't know it.
For flowers were embroidered on it.

Count them.
You may count them. They
Are not like the sand on the sea shore. They
Are not like the multitudes of stars. But single people.
In a corner, in the street.

Yes, count them. Watch them
Watch the sky from their ruins.
Get out from between the stones, and return. Where to
Return? But count them, for they
Serve their term in dreams. And they
Themselves walk outside. Their unbandaged hopes
Are gaping open. In them, they'll die.

Count them.
Too early they learned to read
The terrible writing on the wall. To read and write
On other walls. And the feast went on in silence.

Count them. Be there. For they
Used up all the blood, and there isn't enough,
As in a dangerous operation, when the one is weary
And defeated like a multitude. For who judges
And what is the law, if not
With the full meaning of night
And all the rigor of pity.

⁂ DO NOT ACCEPT ⁂

Do not accept these rains that come too late.
Better to linger. Make your pain
An image of the desert. Say it's said
And do not look to the west. Refuse

To surrender. Try this year too
To live alone in the long summer,
Eat your drying bread, refrain
From tears. And do not learn from

Experience. Take as an example my youth,
My return late at night, what has been written
In the rain of yesteryear. It makes no difference

Now. See your events as my events.
Everything will be as before: Abraham will again
Be Abram. Sarah will be Sarai.

A bright flower bloomed in the old fear.
It's somber spring, spring by the calendar.
Death by choking, death by time,
Death in fire. Death by going far.

What's on the lips—is not in the heart.
And what's all night is not what's at the sea.
Now let us not conceal: everything hurts,
And let the things be said as they may be.

In bitter wrinkles, carved into the world,
Trains travel. Locomotives humming.
Too much destiny for too few people
In the shadow of this earth. They're coming

To pick me up. Where did she go?
More than there was, the echo brings
Me back. The love you don't repeat.
The whirl of the world. The body of lingerings.

Memorial candles in your womb.
Not on a Bible, my hand will take
An oath, but right under your thighs
And under mine. It's somber spring. No break.

And we shall not get excited. Because a translator
May not get excited. Calmly, we shall pass on
Words from man to son, from one tongue
To others' lips, un-

Knowingly, like a father who passes on
The features of his dead father's face
To his son, and he himself is like neither of them.
Merely a mediator.

We shall remember the things we held in our hands
That slipped out.
*What I have in my possession and what I do not have in my possession.*

We must not get excited.
Calls and their callers drowned. Or, my beloved
Gave me a few words before she left,
To bring up for her.

And no more shall we tell what we were told
To other tellers. Silence as admission. We must not
Get excited.

Let the coin decide. Kings
Did so. Do not make up your mind.
Watch how the cloud sings
All you wanted to say or find.

Adorn the chance in words and flowers.
Make policies a trinket for your wife.
Throw away the orders, the summons.
Keep a prayer only, for your life.

Let the streets be your leaders.
Let the moon grow full and play.
Nights are your faithful readers.
Let the thigh. Go all the way.

Build a hut at the corner of Justice.
Let the judge judge his own game.
Count the stars. Sit and do nothing.
And do not ask for his name.

## ➤ HERE ◄

Here, under the kites the children float
High above and those caught by telephone wires
Last year, I stand, the strong branches of my quiet
Decisions grew long ago from my trunk, and the birds
Of small hesitations in my heart, and the rocks
Of the great hesitation at my feet,
And my twin eyes, one always busy and the second
In love. And my gray pants and my green
Sweater, and my face absorbing colors
And returning colors; and I don't know what else
I absorb and return and beam and reject,
And how I was an exchange market for many things.
Export and import. Border post. Junction of roads.
Water divide, divide of the dead. Meeting, parting.

The wind enters the crown of a tree and lingers
In every single leaf; and still, see
How it passes without pause—
And we come, pause for a while, and fall.
Like among sisters, a lot of similarity in the world:
Thighs and mountainsides. A distant thought
Is like the actions that grew here
In the flesh and in the mountains, like cypress trees
Happening darkly on the ridge.
The cycle is closed. I am its buckle.

But until I discovered that my hard fathers
Were soft inside, my fathers died.
All the generations preceding me are acrobats
Riding on one another's back
In a circus, and I am mostly beneath
All of them, with the big load on my shoulders.
Sometimes I'm at the peak: one hand raised
To the roof, and the applause in the arena
Is my own prize and flesh.

1

In lions' lair of sand,
So truly at the sea,
In evening's tent, all tanned.
To be, again to be.

Invented you, first-rate,
Dream Bedouin, my stunt.
Come let us devastate
The night, the thighs, the cunt.

Account for checks, deposits,
Returns always proper.
My multiplied composite:
A carbon paper copy.

The law of out and in,
Who held you so as me?
Am I under your skin
By a majority?

Decisive to the finish,
Sleep architect of scope,
The shore will not diminish
You model of my hope.

Conditionally naked,
Suntanned, of now, of prime,
In spasm of sand we make it
Quietly. You had time

And I the hasty urge,
Your shoulders showed perhaps

Ship's route, how to diverge—
Without the shoulder-straps.

Shelves of desire. A niche
For yearnings. A hot counter.
A window for the fish,
For bad dreams. And I mount her.

Redoubt without a doubt.
Of thoughts, barely a trace.
Identity about
Your lap, your autumn face.

Clothes scattered in the blitz
In sand their color pales
And grass between the tits
And lovely crevice snails.

Blood with no flesh in sight
Hot gravel like a vandal.
Will we recall the flight
Of an unbuckled sandal?

## 2

So truly at the sea
Out of my ways and wings,
Did you go out to be
Beyond all living things?

You come, return again
Like seashells scattered loose
Dream muscles gone insane
In night of the canoes.

Your seaweed ear that smells,
Putrescent wood will bend.
Unfurl your belly sails.
The purpose of our end.

A whirlpool of crabs,
A navel of forgetting,
All time is up for grabs,
An effortless resetting.

An absent mindful love
In yesteryear's abode,
Words not to be removed
In the past mode.

The sand of bodies sprawled
Upon the wandering flesh
And laughter that unrolled
Old cries, still sharp and fresh.

A ghetto made of love,
A distance with no veil.
Hope of a stable-dove,
Vain goal with no avail.

Plan of a lighthouse scene,
A contour of the self,
A model of tanned skin
Of the hellenic shelf.

A seashore polyglot
Who wrings the necks of kings.
Sun with no man, a spot
Without a road. All swings.

Shall we continue? All
It was, you never met.
A tower in the fall,
A Jaffa minaret.

A tempest in the hair,
Unprecedented flesh.
We waited for the flair
The east wind will enmesh.

A lair of sandy nerves,
Forgetful womb, a shrine.
A track that slightly curves.
The bottom line.


3

So truly at the sea,
Will we yet meet, and where?
Incense of guilty plea
And honey of despair.

As ripe as watermelons
Without a gardener's glance,
In thousand fields: we felons
Of such a hasty dance.

A daily unpaid hand
For memorizing all—
The words, the moves, the sand
I shall recall.

Dream window of display—
My soul to touch and see,
Homeland of cry and play,
Childhood of prophecy.

At first you're mine, you're my
Penultimately stressed,
And later, riding high
In carriage of your dress.

Of Hebron glass your eyes,
Archaeological.
Black rage your hair. Face nice,
A gate to wait and call.

When did you leave at all?
And me, did you see me?

The secret of my scroll,
The slander of the sea.

You hyperbolic temple,
You ruin child that feels,
Wild card of run and trample,
And orange peels.

A girl abandonee,
Clouds' granddaughter so wild,
You seaweed progeny,
You peanut child.

Hot flesh, proverbial
Of bad and good and shoddy,
You fooled my full recall
With a wet body.

As hard as ancient coins,
Your screwing so precise,
Your celebrating loins,
Neck-wringing thighs.

Your navel filled with sand
And crystallizing salt,
A temple remnant, grand
Your foaming head, no fault.

A circus of our bones,
A lair of selfish I's,
A human beast in groans
The death of all four thighs.

In shadow, honey feet,
Two moons of buttocks free.
Let chill of idols meet
Bare-cover mystery.

Imperative of will
In body of the double,
And sins for both to fill,
And finish in a rubble.

And shall I add: I do
Not see you in the sand
And after all, to woo
And understand.

From here, it looks: gray hue,
Essential as to be.
And you, have you
Remained with me?

Don't prepare for tomorrow. Turn your face to the narrow alley,
Turn to dream, stairs will lead you, cover your plans
In sand, like shed blood. Break the roads
Even before the sharp curve, which breaks them anyway.

And what was lent to your body, your blood, return it: it won't stay.
Water will be changed for flowers,
Wine will pass, like life leaving a person,
Knocking at the gate. Don't open, stay
Inside. Sit in the dark, stand in the place
Where the murmur of worshipers is like the murmur of the sea waves.
Don't get close to find out what it is. This is the place.
Don't move. You passed.
You wept. You smiled. You had your picture taken.

See little girls jumping rope: the fate of a rope
Beaten to the ground and rising again like a gate above them.
Don't disturb now. Stand on the side.
Revolve, turn, buy yourself a slave in the wind. Push
The world back like a swimmer with arms and legs. It will
Hit the face of the water and hurt it, but will leave
You above among the living. Don't cut yourself off. Into the lap
Weep the future of your life. Sit a long time facing
The face of woman. Don't speak. This too is prophecy.
On the slope, love the stone placed under the wheel
To stop, like yourself, the rolling time.

And in the gates of houses don't erase the names
Of the dead from the sign. Those not alive are here too.
Even if they are already carved on tombstones. Let their names
Be double: there and here.

And the horrible doors, slowly
Closing on you, don't let them
Close on you. Wedge anything between the jamb and the closing:

A shoe, your hand, last words. It hurts. But it
Will sustain you.
Test your new feelings, outside,
Like a new weapon, far from the last houses,
In a closed valley, early, in total dawn.

And be like your mother on the Sabbath eve,
Blocking between her and her candles.
Then take away, like her, the blocking hand
And bless only if you know that everything remained
And is really yours.
Then bless.

Save me, O God; for the waters are come in onto my soul.
I sink in deep mire, where there is no standing: I am come into
deep waters, where the floods overflow me. —PSALM 69, 1–3


I know how high the flooding waters came
Last winter. But I do not know how high
Love came inside me. Perhaps it overflowed
My banks. For what remained on the steep slopes
Of the dry riverbed?—Just crusted mire.
And on my face?—Not even the white line
On the lips of a child who drank his milk
And put the clinking glass on the bright counter.
What's left? Perhaps a leaf inside a stone
Placed on the window sill for our protection,
An angel, when we are inside. To love is
Not to remain. Nor to leave a trace. To change
Entirely. Forgotten. To understand
Is to flourish. The spring understands.
To remember my beloved is to forget
All the acquired property. To love
Is to forget the other love, to close
All other doors. See, we saved a place,
We left a coat, a book, on the empty seat,
Perhaps, empty forever. And how long
Can we reserve it? For they'll come, a stranger
Will sit near you. Impatiently, you turn
Back, to the door with a red sign, glance at
Your watch—a habit like a kiss, a prayer.
Outside, they always make up new ideas,
Put them on weary faces, like colored light.
Or see the child, his thoughts painted on him
Like on an ancient vase in an exhibit
For others, not yet thinking for himself.
The land is wandering under our feet
Like a revolving stage or like your face,

I thought they're mine, but weren't. But the child
Was lost. Last scion of his games, grandchild
Of ancient hiding places, he went out,
His toys were ringing among hollow wells,
After the holidays, an awesome cycle
Of calls and silence, hope and death and hope.
And everybody searched, happy to seek
In the land of forgetting: voices, an air-
Plane, flying low like thoughts, police dogs
With philosophical faces, question marks
Frolicking on skinny legs among the grass
Drying before our eyes. Words used in prayers,
Talks, papers, Jeremiahs on all fours.

And demonstrations clogged the streets of cities,
Like a clogged heart, its owner dying. And
The dead hung out for their eternal ripening
In the history of the world. They sought
The child, and found some couples, hidden lovers,
Found jugs from ancient times, and all that wished
Not to be found. For love there was too short,
It didn't cover all, like a short blanket,
A head or legs protruded in the wind
When cold night came. Or others found a shortcut
Of sharp, short pain, instead of avenues,
Long and repressing joy and happiness.
At night, there were the names of all the world,
Of foreign cities, somber lakes and peoples
Who vanished from the world long ago.
And all the names are like the name of my beloved.
She raised her head to listen. She imagined
They called her, yet they didn't look for her.
The child has vanished. You could see the paths
On the distant mountain. Little time left.
Olives spoke heavy stones. In the great fear
Between the sky and ground, new houses rose,
Their window panes chilling the flaming forehead
Of a hot night. The wind in the dry grass
Shot up like preying beasts. The absentminded

Mutual lucidity erected
High bridges in the wasteland. Traps were set,
Projectors lit, and nets of hair were stretched
In warp and woof. But they passed by the place
And didn't see; the child hid, curled up
Among the stones for buildings of tomorrow.
Eternal paper rustled between their legs.
In print, and not in print. The orders were
Heard clearly. Numbers were precise: not ten
Or fifty, but twenty-seven, thirty-one,
Or forty-three, so we can be believed.

At dawn, the search resumed: Fast, faster, here!
I saw him among the toys of his wells,
His pebble games, his olive arms. I heard
His heart beat under a rock. He's there. He's here.
The tree has moved a bit. You didn't see?
And new calls, as an ancient sea brings ships
With loud calls to a foreign shore. And we
Returned to our cities, where a great
Tristesse is shared in equal parts, well spaced,
Like mailbox blocks, for us to drop our need:
A name and address, and the emptying time.
The stones sang in a choir of black mouths
Into the earth, the boy heard it, not we.
For he was lingering more than ourselves,
Face posing for a cloud, and memorized
By sons of olives, not leaving any trace,
Like love, as one of them entirely.
Because to love is not to remain. To be
Forgotten. Disappear. But God remembered,
Like a man returning to the first place
To recall what he forgot, God has
Come back to our small room, to try and recall
How He meant to build His world with love.
Did not forget our names. For names are not
Forgotten. If we call a shirt, a shirt
For many days—though used to sweep the dust—
It's still a shirt, perhaps it is the old shirt.

How long will we continue thus? For we
Are changing. Yet the name remains. What is
Our right to bear our names, to call the Jordan
Jordan, after it passed through Lake Kineret.
Who is he? The same that entered Capernaum?
Who are we, after we passed an awesome love?
Who is the Jordan? Who remembers? Boats with
Tourists have left. The mountains opposite
Are mute: Susita, Hermon, the terrifying
Arbel, the town of pain, Tiberias.

Now everyone will disregard the names,
The rules of the game, the hollow calls.
An hour passes, the barber cuts your hair,
Door opens. And the rest for broom and street.
The barber bends, his watch close to your ear.
This too is time. End time, perhaps. The child
Not found. The rain's effect, though it is summer,
Seen all around. And from earth's dream, the trees
Speak loudly. In the wind, tin sounds resound.
We slept together. When I went: the eyes
Of my beloved gaped in fear. She rose
In bed, leaned on her elbows. The white sheet,
Pure white as Judgment Day. She couldn't stay
At home alone, went out into the world
That started on the stairs beyond her door.
But the child stayed, and it began to look
Like winds, like trunks of olive trees, like mountains.
Such family resemblances: the face of
One who fell in the Negev will appear
As the face of his cousin in New York.
A mountain rift in Arava appears
In the face of a broken friend. A ridge
And night, resemblance and tradition. A night's
Custom that has become the law of lovers.
Temporary precautions are permanent.
Police, calls outside, dialogues internal
Within our human bodies. Fire trucks
Sound no alarm on their way back from fires.

Returning quietly from ash and ember.
We too returned calmly from the valley
After the search and love: as overlooked.
But some of us went on to listen. It seemed
Someone called out. Extending our ear's shell
With a round hand, we stretched our heart's space too
With one more love, to better hear and better
To forget.

        The child died on that night,
Clean, neatly combed. Well tended, licked by tongues
Of God and night. "When we arrived here, it
Was light, now it is dark." All clean and white,
A sheet of paper in an envelope.
Enshrined in books of Psalms of the land of the dead.
Some still continued searching, or sought pain
To match their weeping or joy for their laughter,
Everything does not match everything.
Even the hands are from another body.
It seemed to us, however, something dropped:
We heard the clanking, like a coin that fell.
We stood. We turned around. Bent down to the ground.
Not found. Each one went on his way.

# Now in the Din
## Before the Silence

✻⟶✻⟶✻⟶ ⟵✻⟵✻⟵✻

1963–1968

# Poems of Jerusalem

## ❧ JERUSALEM 1967 ❧

1

*For my friends Dennis,*
*Arye, and Harold*

This year I traveled far away
To see the tranquillity of my city.
A baby is calmed by rocking, a city is calmed by distance.
I lived in longing. I played the game
Of Yehuda Halevy's four strict squares:
My heart. Myself. East. West.*

I heard bells ringing with the faiths of the times,
But the wailing I heard inside me
Was always of my desert Yehuda.

Now that I have returned, I scream again.
And at night, stars rise like bubbles of people drowning,
Every morning I scream like a newborn babe
At the confusion of houses and all this great light.

2

I returned to this city where names
Were given to distances as to human beings
And numbers not of bus lines,
But 70 After, 1917, five hundred
Before the Common Era, forty-eight. Those are the lines
You travel in for real.

And now the ghosts of the past meet
The ghosts of the future and discuss me above me,
Give and take, don't give and don't take,
In high trajectories of cartridges over my head.

*An allusion to the opening of Yehuda Halevy's Zionist poem written in Spain:
  "My heart is in the East, and myself at the end of the West."

A person returning to Jerusalem feels that places
That were painful no longer hurt.
But a slight warning remains in everything,
Like a light swaying veil: warning.


3

Lighted Tower of David, lighted Church of the Virgin,
Lighted forefathers sleeping in the Cave of Makhpelah,*
Faces lighted from inside, lighted transparent
Honey cakes, lighted clock and lighted time
Passing through your thighs as you take off your dress.

Lighted lighted. Lighted cheeks of my childhood,
Lighted stones that would be lighted together
With those who would sleep in dark squares.

Lighted balustrade spiders and webs of churches
And winding staircases. But of all of them, in all of them,
The lighted X-ray writing, terrible, real,
In letters of bones, in white and lightning: *Mene, mene,*
*Thou art weighed in the balances and found wanting.*


4

In vain do you seek the barbed wire fences.
You know such things
Do not disappear. Another city perhaps
Is now cut in two: two lovers
Separated; other flesh is tormented now
With these thorns, refuses to be stone.

In vain do you seek. *You lift up your eyes unto the hills,*
Perhaps there? Not these hills, accidents of geology,
But the Hills. You raise questions
Without raising your pitch, without a question mark,
To meet the obligation of questions.


*The burial cave of the Patriarchs in Hebron.

And there are none. But a great weariness wants you with all your desire
And receives. Like death.

Jerusalem, only city in the world
Where even the dead are given voting rights.


## 5

On Yom Kippur in the year of forgetting, TaShKaH,* I put on
Dark festive clothes and went to the Old City in Jerusalem.
I stood a long time before the niche of an old Arab store,
Not far from Nablus Gate, a store
Of buttons and zippers and spools of thread
Of every color and snaps and buckles.
Dear light and many colors, like an open Ark of the Covenant.

In my heart I told him that my father too
Had such a store of threads and buttons.
In my heart I explained to him about all the dozens of years
And causes and accidents, that I am here now
And my father's store was burned there and he is buried here.

When I finished, it was closing time, the closing prayer.
He too put down the shutter and locked the gate
And I returned home with all the worshipers.


## 6

Not time that distances me from my childhood
But this city and everything in it. Now
To learn Arabic too, to get to Jericho
From both sides of time. And the length of added walls
And the height of towers and domes of temples
Of boundless surface. All those
Broaden my life and force me
Always to emigrate again from the smell
Of rivers and forests.


*Year beginning in the fall of 1967, after the Six-Day War; the acronym also means
"You will forget."

My life is stretched like this. It becomes very thin
And transparent as fabric. You can see through me.

7

In this summer of open-eyed hatred
And blind love, I begin again to believe
In all the small things that will fill
The craters of mortar shells: earth and some grass,
And after the rain perhaps, every creeping thing.
I think of children growing half in the ethics of their fathers
And half in the teachings of war.
The tears penetrate my eyes now from outside
And every day my ears invent the footsteps of the herald.

8

The city plays hide-and-seek among its names:
Yerushalayim, Al-Kuds, Salem, Jeru, Yeru,
Whispers: Jebus, Jebus, Jebus, in the dark.
Weeps with longing: *Aelia Capitolina, Aelia, Aelia.*
She comes to everyone who calls
Lonely at night. But we know
Who came to whom.

9

On the open door, a sign: "Closed."
How do you explain this? Now
The chain is loose on both sides: No
Jailed or jailer, no dog and no master.
The chain will soon turn into wings.
How do you explain this?
You will explain this.

10

Jerusalem is low, crouching between her mountains,
Not like New York, for example.
Two thousand years ago, she crouched
In a wonderful lunge.
All other cities ran great
Circles in the arena of time, won or lost,

And died. Jerusalem remained in a lunge:
All victories are taut and concealed in her. All defeats.
Her strength grows and her breath is calm
For a race even outside the arena.


## 11

Loneliness is always in the middle,
Defended and fortified. People should have
Felt confidence in that and they don't.
When they leave after long lingering,
Caves for new hermits are opened.
What do you know about Jerusalem.
You don't have to understand languages;
They traverse everything as through ruins.
Human beings are a wall of moving stones.
But even in the Western Wall
I didn't see stones as sad as those.
My pain is lit in all its letters like the name of the hotel opposite.
What awaits me and what doesn't await me. Amen.


## 12

Jerusalem stone is the only stone
That feels pain. It has a nervous system.
From time to time Jerusalem congregates
Into a mass of protest like the Tower of Babel.
But God-Police hits with big clubs:
Houses are ruined, walls breached,
And then the city will scatter again, murmuring
Prayers of complaint and screams-here-and-there from churches
And synagogues and moaning minarets.
Everyone to his own place.


## 13

Near destroyed houses and crooked
Iron, like arms of the dead, you will always find
Somebody sweeping the paved path
Or arranging the little garden, sensitive
Paths, square flowerbeds.
Great wishes for strange death are well-tended

As in the monastery of the White Brothers near Lions' Gate.
But a little farther, in the yard, the soil is gaping:
Pillars and vaults bear soil in vain
And negotiations with each other, Crusaders and Ministering Angels,
Sultan and Rabbi Yehuda Hasid. Arched vaults with
Pillars, ransom of prisoners and strange conditions in rolled
Contracts and stone seals. Twisted hooks holding
Air.
Cornices and fragments of pillars strewn like chess pieces
In a game abandoned in rage,
And Herod who hissed two thousand years ago
Like mortar shells. He knew.

### 14

If clouds are the ceiling, I like to
Sit in the room underneath. A dead Kingdom rising
Above me like vapors rising from a warm dish.
A door rasps: a cloud opens.
In distant valleys someone struck iron on stone
But the echo raises great and different things in the air.

On top of the houses—houses with houses on top of them. This is
All of history.
Learning like this in schools with no roof
And no walls and no bench and no teachers. Learning
Like this in the absolute outside,
Learning brief as one heartbeat. Everything.

### 15

I and Jerusalem like the blind and the lame.
She sees for me
Up to the Dead Sea, up to the End of Days.
And I ride her on my shoulders
And walk blind in my darkness below.

### 16

On this bright autumn day
I am founding Jerusalem anew.

Founding scrolls
Fly in the air, birds, thoughts.

God is furious with me
Because I force Him always
To create the world anew
From chaos, light, second day, until
Man, and back again.

### 17

In the morning the shadow of the Old City
Falls on the new. Afternoon—the opposite.
No one gains. The muezzin's prayer
Is wasted on the new houses. The pealing
Of bells rolls and bounces like balls.
The holy scream from synagogues will fade like gray smoke.

At the end of summer, I breathe this air,
Burned and hurting. Silence.
Thought like many closed books:
Many crowded books, most of their pages
Stuck together like eyelids in the morning.

### 18

I climb up the Tower of David
A little above the rising prayer,
Halfway to the sky. Some
Of the ancients succeeded: Mohammed, Jesus,
Others. But they didn't find rest in the sky,
They fell into a heavenly excitement. Yet
The applause for them hasn't stopped since then
Down on earth.

### 19

Jerusalem is built on varied foundations
Of restrained scream. If there is no reason
For the scream, the foundations will break, the city crumble.
If the scream screams, Jerusalem will burst to the sky.

## 20

At evening, poets come to the Old City
And leave it laden with images
And metaphors and little thought parables
And twilight similes from among the niches and cornices,
From ripe fruit
And filigree of the heart.

I lifted my hand to my forehead
To wipe the sweat
And caught Else Lasker-Schüler,
By accident. Light and lonely she was in her life,
Let alone in her death. But her poems!

## 21

Jerusalem a port on the shore of eternity.
The Temple Mount a huge ship, luxury cruise liner.
From the portholes of her Western Wall peer jolly
Saints, the passengers. Hasids on the platform wave
Goodbye, shout hurray see you. The ship
Always arrives, always sails off. And the fences and piers
And the police and the banners and the tall masts of churches
And mosques and the smokestacks of synagogues and the boats
Of praise and the waves of mountains. Voice of the Shofar is heard: one
More sailed off. Yom Kippur sailors in white uniforms
Scale ladders and ropes of tested prayers.

And the give and take and the gates and the golden domes:
Jerusalem is the Venice of God.

## 22

Jerusalem is a sister city to Sodom.
But the merciful salt didn't have mercy on her
And didn't cover her with quiet white.
Jerusalem is a refusing Pompeii.
History books tossed into the fire,
Their pages curling, hardening in red.

An eye too bright, blind,
Always breaks in a sieve of veins.
Many births gaping below,
A womb with boundless teeth,
Woman of many mouths double-edged and holy beasts.

The sun thought Jerusalem was a sea
And sank in it by awful mistake.
Fish of the sky were caught in a net of alleys,
Tearing each other like fish.

Jerusalem. An operation left open.
The surgeons went off to sleep in distant skies.
But her dead fall into line
Little by little, all around
Like quiet petals.
My God!
My rod!

My child wafts peace.
When I lean over him,
It is not just the smell of soap.

All the people were children wafting peace.
(And in the whole land, not even one
Millstone remained that still turned.)

Oh, the land torn like clothes
That can't be mended.
Hard, lonely fathers even in the cave of the Makhpelah.
Childless silence.

My child wafts peace.
His mother's womb promised him
What God cannot
Promise us.

## ALL THE GENERATIONS
BEFORE ME


All the generations before me contributed me
Little by little so I will emerge here in Jerusalem
All at once, like a prayer house or a philanthropy.
That compels. My name is the name of my contributors.
That compels.

I approach the age of my father's death.
My will has many patches,
I have to change my life and my death
Day by day, to fulfill all the prophecies
That prophesied me. So they won't be a lie.
That compels.

I passed my fortieth year. There are jobs
I cannot get. If I were in Auschwitz
They wouldn't have sent me to work,
They would have burned me right away.
That compels.

When was the last time I cried.
The time has come to collect evidence
From those who caught me at it. Some are dead.
I wash my eyes with water
To see again the world
Through a wet and painful veil. I need
To collect evidence. These days
For the first time, I have felt pangs
In my heart:
I wasn't scared. I was almost as proud as a boy
Discovering the first hair in his armpits
And his groin.

My mother always calls me in
From playing outside. Once she called me
And I didn't return for many years,
And not from playing.

When I sit before her now
She is like silent stones.
All my words and my poems
Are like the greased outpouring of words
Of a carpet merchant,
A pimp, and a smooth traveling salesman.

In mid-advance
It turned into retreat. But
The direction of the march
Did not change. Suddenly.

The seams burst.
The hoarder I was,
Collector,
All I collected drops off on the road.
You can follow me easily,
I am scattered.

But something of my village forefathers
Remained inside me:
When I want now, this evening, to gather
Something, not cattle, not flocks.
To gather something.

I will have to begin to remember you
When someone else begins to discover you, the inside
Of your soft thighs above the stockings and when you laugh,
Developing the first pictures for his future dreams.

And I will have to forget you
When someone else begins to remember you
When some other elses begin to discover you.

And my life is empty like a flower when they plucked
All its petals: yes, no, yes, no, yes.

And to be alone is to be in a place
Where we were never together, and to be alone is
To forget you are like this: to want to pay for two
In a bus and travel alone.

Now I shall cover the mirror like your pictures
And lie down to sleep. The birds of the sky will eat
The flesh of my sleep. The dogs will lick
My blood inside. You won't see a thing outside.

Caught in the homeland-trap of a Chosen People.
A Cossack fur hat on your head, you—
Offspring of their pogroms. *After those things,*
As ever.
For example, your face: slanted eyes
Of sixteen-forty-eight, forty-nine, thine. High
Cheekbones of a Hetman, chief plunderer,
But the mitzvah dance of Hasidim.
Naked on a rock at dusk,
Under the water canopies of Eyn Gedi,
With closed eyes and a body open like hair. After
Those things, *as ever.*

Caught in a homeland-trap:
To talk now in this tired tongue,
Torn out of its sleep in the Bible: blinded,
It totters from mouth to mouth. In a tongue that described
Miracles and God, now to say: automobile, bomb, God.

The square letters wanted to remain
Closed; every letter a locked house,
To remain and to be enclosed in a final D
And sleep in it forever.

# ✦ LUXURY ✦

My uncle is buried in Sheikh Badr, my other uncle
Scattered in the Carpathian Mountains. My father is buried in Sanhedria,
My grandmother on the Mount of Olives. And all their fathers' fathers
Are buried in a half-destroyed Jewish graveyard
In the villages of lower Franconia,
Near rivers and forests that are not Jerusalem.

My grandfather, who converted cows with heavy eyes
In the shed under the kitchen and got up at four in the morning.
This early rising I inherited from him. With a mouth bitter
From nightmares, I foster my bad dreams.

Grandfather, grandfather, Chief Rabbi of my life,
Sell my pains, as you sold
Leavened dough before Passover: let them remain in me
And even pain me,
But not be mine. Not in my possession.

So many graves are scattered in the past of my life,
Names engraved like the names of canceled railroad stations.

How will I cover all the distances with my roads,
How will I link all of them? Such an expensive railroad system
I cannot afford to maintain. Luxury.

Last evening I gave you the parable
Of my father, who on the eve of Passover eve
Would slice bread carefully
Into precise cubes and put them
On the window sill so he would be able
To find them with his heavy eyes
In the light of a candle dancing a mitzvah dance.
So his blessing on the burning of leavened bread
Would not be in vain.

To live like this:
Stage directors of ourselves,
Cheating directors
With perfect faith, almost,
And we shall not be
In vain.

## MY SON, MY SON,
## MY HEAD, MY HEAD

My son, my son, my head, my head,
In this train, I pass
Through alien landscape, reading of Auschwitz
And learning about the difference
Between "to leave" and "not to remain."

My son, my head, my head, my son,
The roads are wet like a drowned woman
Pulled out of the river at dawn
After a wild search with crazy lights.
Now silence:
Shining dead body.

My head, my head, my son, my son!
The inability to define your pain precisely
Impedes the doctors from diagnosing an illness.
It means we can never
Really love.

Lots of grapes this year,
But no peace in my heart. I eat them
Like a crazy bird among scarecrows.

The smell of last fruit turned into smell of wine
Not to drink. Now to bless
Even the last ones. *That you made us live and exist and reach*
*This* last *time.* Grapes,
Big and black, turned my mouth into the inside of a woman.
Your lips discovered an overripe fig and will remain so
Even in winter. People explained bright landscapes
Of summer's end, but I thought of my love
That's not enough to cover this big land.

It was a long year, full of fruit and corpses.
More than ever, we await the rain.
Lots of grapes this year, the last ones are yellow
Like wasps carrying their own death inside.

The second year of drought, and no love.
Now I go north
To spend my last moisture
In settled places.
The women there have fat behinds,
Their belly button sinks deeper into their belly.
Mine is exposed and stands out from the receding, hoarse flesh.

The hair has turned white on my chest:
The animal inside me grows old before my head turns gray.

I am sad granaries of seed
And the seed too
Bears the sadness of every living, every dead.
Dark corpses of thoughts and echo.

Round wells stuck
Like male organs deep in the earth,
Full of water or teeming with serpents and scorpions, cruel
Seed.

Black tents to the horizon.
Upturned tent, black triangle above my groin.
Words greet me with barking.

The end of my peace. Hard lust
Rises like towers of beckoning cities,
But my words remain soft
As the lamb's wool I left there.

No house accepted us.
Like a tent, I stretched myself above you,
Like a straw mat,
I spread myself beneath you.
Your red dress opened like a chalice to the sky,
When you sat on me erect as on a saddle
To save your thighs from the hard ground.

"Meshugga," you said in your foreign tongue:
His dog died on the leash.
His friends are far away.
His son dreams of saying Kaddish.

## PITY, WE WERE A
## GOOD INVENTION

They amputated
Your thighs from my waist.
For me they are always
Surgeons. All of them.

They dismantled us
One from another. For me they are engineers.
Pity. We were a good and loving

Invention: an airplane made of man and woman,
Wings and all:
We soared a bit from the earth,
We flew a bit.

**1**

I resign.
My son already has my father's eyes,
My mother's hands,
My mouth.
No need for me.
Thank you.

The refrigerator starts humming,
Ready for a long journey.
A strange dog weeps for the loss of someone else.
I resign.

**2**

I paid dues to so many funds.
I'm overinsured.
I'm tied up and entangled with everybody.
Every change in my life will cost them a lot of money.
My every move will hurt them,
My death will wipe them out.
And my voice is passing with the clouds.
My outstretched hand turned into paper: one more contract.
I see the world through yellow roses—
Someone forgot them
On my table at the window.

**3**

Bankruptcy!
I declare the whole world
A womb.
From this moment on, I abandon myself
And deposit myself in it:
Let it adopt me. Let it worry!

*Yehuda Amichai*

I declare the president of the United States
My father, and the premier of the Soviet Union
The trustee of my assets, and the British Cabinet
My family, and Mao Zedong my grandmother.
They must all help me!
I resign.
I declare the sky God.
Let them all together do to me
What I didn't believe they would do.

# Poems of Caesarea

*from*
→ POEMS ON THE SHORE ←
OF CAESAREA

### 4

The weary salt said: Here
They are again, the two who want
To be covered with the taste of salt.
Their own taste isn't enough for them.
Their own salt isn't enough,
Or their own love.
They come here often
Not to forget. They will forget.

### 5

And so we live here. Like the sea,
Separating things that are better preserved
From things that are less.
"What should we take with us?"
"Next year I'll still wear that."
"When will we stop loving?" Our friends
Have retreated inside the brown country.
The hand raised to wave goodbye—
What does it feel when it returns
To the side of the calmed body, what happened
To it on the way? What do we get from knowledge
About the Crusaders or Romans or other gilded conquerors
Who built this crumbling black port?
The knowledge pleases our ears
Like the dance tune on the soft and sandy
Loudspeaker. History as entertainment
In the empty afternoon hours at the sea,

Like us, separating the better preserved from the less.
How long is the fossil rock? And the black marble?
How long is next year?
How long is the limestone, loving as it crumbles,
And the sand that lives forever and for the wind in its death.

### 6

I swam alone far away
Beyond the jetty, and suddenly I stopped moving,
Like ships standing in mid-sea
And their agitated passengers don't know the reason.
Not from weariness did it come to me. The sea was still
And I was strong. I thought about the senselessness
Of return. Why should a man return to the shore?
I saw it yellow and gray, not like land,
But like a horizon. Like the horizon in the west,
Drawing with a thin line the beginning of other distances.
Why should I return?

Then something again began beating inside me
Like a dull motor shaking the ship.
It was oblivion that began beating inside me:
A motor much stronger than the needs of my life,
Greater than my body, mightier than all my memories.
It bears me far away, beyond my death.

### 7

The woman that disappeared beyond
The door marked "Women" and never came out again.
The sand between my toes.
Half an apple and a quarter of an hour, coming late.
A ticket with the wound of a precise voyage,
A number on a forearm, half a burned match.
Anointed skin. For whom?

Red sinners stand
In the hellfire of a shower
And scream to lust for help.
Two round men rolling

On boards of mud, like a printing press.
Cornhusks and dried pomegranates
In the bowl of a lap.

Somebody whispers with a mouthful of sand:
"Like the sand on the seashore."
A woman enters her dress
As ascending a ladder. Her face afire.


### 8

The sea preserves in salt,
Jerusalem preserves in dryness.
Where shall we go?
Now, in the precise evenings, to choose:
Not what to do and how to live,
But to choose a life
Whose dreams will hurt less
In all the nights to come.


### 9

Come again next winter,
Or some such words,
Sustain my life
And pass my days,
Like a line of soldiers, one by one, over the bridge
Marked for blowing up.

Come again next winter.
Who didn't hear such words, and who will return?

My mother once told me
Not to sleep with flowers in the room.
Ever since, I don't sleep
With flowers, I sleep
Alone, without them.

There were lots of flowers,
But I never had enough time.
And beloved people push off
From my life,
Like boats from the shore.

My mother told me
Not to sleep with flowers:
Don't sleep. The mother of my childhood
Won't sleep.

The wooden banister I clutched
When they dragged me off to school
Was burned down long ago.
But my clutching hands remained
Clutching.

# THE ANNIVERSARY OF
## MY FATHER'S DEATH

When the moon is full,
The anniversary for my father. Always.

Never will the day of his death occur
In a summer or a spring.

I put little stones on his grave:
A sign I was here,
A visiting card of the living at the stone,

The big stone of my father. My father
The cause and the effect,
Your alarm clock breaks my body.

The two Sabbath candles of my mother
Travel softly side by side in the street,
Pulled by a ship
I never saw.

From a hollow echoing gym
High shrieks,
Steam and someone else's sweat
With the smell of rubber and girls' thighs.

Father, now I love to wash and comb my hair,
But otherwise I haven't changed.

The scraps of information about you on the tombstone,
Less than a passport.

There is no police station to
Turn myself in as a murderer.

*Yehuda Amichai*

When I get home, I shall lie on my back
With my arms spread, as crucified.

That calms me,
Father.

# THE HEART IS A CORRUPT
## STAGE DIRECTOR

The last days of summer are
The last days of two together.
The heart is a corrupt stage director.

Separate separates from separate.
And in the nights the writing says: nights.
Despair that despaired of us
Turned into hope.

I think that Newton too discovered
Whatever he discovered in the intermission
Between two pains.
What shall we learn from this about the excitement of our lives,
What shall we learn about the quiet words
Surrounding it? What things
Have to fall from a tree for us to learn?

It is terrible to fight
Love with sleeping pills. What have we come to?

This place will not console us.
This place.
On the ground of a great thirst
Lie the houses of the city. Great rifts in the earth
From my screaming your name
Till my eyes hurt.

He who changes himself changes his place,
Even if he stays there. This place
Will not console us.
The light patches on the dark, ancient, reconstructed vase:
What is new in me and what is from my forefathers?
For we are yesterday, for we are of others.
Shadows pass over our faces, shadows pass
Through us. This night too
Is the shadow of another world.

In my worst dreams
You always appear with light eyes next to
Walls whose cornerstone is: heart

Of all the things I do, one
Is always to say farewell. In my dreams
I hear a voice, not my voice
And not your voice, and not your echo.

Wrinkled eyes of weary wild animals, my eyes.
The lust of days that passed with their nights.

And until my death I must remember the heavy
Smell of figs, like the heavy eyes of my father.
The fig tree is a very Jewish tree.

Now they cast of my face a mask of love, as they cast
A death mask. They cast, and I didn't feel it,
When I lay next to you loving: my true face.

I am big and fat.
For every pound of fat
I add a pound of sadness.

I was a great stammerer, but since
I have learned to lie, my speech ripples like water.
Only my face has remained heavy
Like unpronounceable syllables,
Stumbling blocks, stammer.

Sometimes my eyes still flash
As from the fire of weapons, very far
Inside me. An old battle.

I demand of others
Not to forget, I myself want to forget,
In the end, am forgotten.

When Moses sat
With God on Mount Sinai and wrote
On the tablets,
I sat in the back of the class, in a corner
And drew, dreaming,
Flowers and faces, airplanes
And embellished names.

Now I'll show you everything:
Do not do and do not listen!

## ➤ HIRBET SAYID ◄

The flowering of the oak blurs
This precise and strict tree, like foam,
Like dreams. We called the name of each plant,
We distinguished one flower from another, and from the carving on a
    stone,
As then, in Hirbet Sayid.

The wristwatch in my shoe, the shoe in the grass,
No payment and no reparation, no memory and no forefathers
And their lands. Grass like hair and hair like grass,
In Hirbet Sayid.

We were sad with the layers beneath us,
A khan and a fortress, Crusader and Roman, stone and lime,
Dust and dust.
We were happy with the layers above us,
Already marked by an archaeologist
Of a future not ours, layers of happiness
Unused, calls and their callers, air not breathed,
As then in Hirbet Sayid.

When after hours of walking
You suddenly discover
That the body of the woman striding beside you
Is not made for
A march or war,

That her thighs grow heavy
And her buttocks move like a tired flock,
You are filled with great joy
For the world
Where women are like this.

They closed the Jaffa port.
My love, close the doors of the sea!
In my childhood, they dressed me on the Sabbath
In a sailor shirt over the four ritual fringes
And a sailor hat on my head.
My parents weren't thinking of a sea and ships.
Now you close the sea and its doors.
The warehouses are empty. My love is with me.
In the evening sadness, someone suddenly says: "Women
With hoarse voices love more." Not to interpret,
Not to explain these words.
Close the doors of the sea.

My child is so sad.
I teach him:
Geography of loves,
Foreign languages he cannot hear
Because of the distance.

My child shakes his little bed up to me
At night. I teach him.
More than forgetting. The language of forgetting.
By the time he understands my deeds, I'll be dead.

What are you doing with our quiet child?
You cover  him with a blanket,
Like the sky. A layer of clouds.
I could have been the moon.

What are you doing with your sad fingers?
You cover them with a glove
And leave.
I was the moon.

✦ HYMN TO SUMMER ✦

These days, God leaves the earth,
To go to His summer house
In the dark mountains that are you,
And leaves us to the hot wind, the sword, and envy.

Let us not say too much. Let us not be
Too much. Eternity is a perfect
Form of mutual loneliness.

A sweet feeling between our legs
Tells us of the weakness of lingering
And of the sadness of words to say.

# ➤ IN THOSE DAYS, ⬥
## IN THIS TIME

*Those days* separate slowly
From *this time*, like a guard returning to his place,
Like mourners returning from a funeral to their distant home.

Remember? "I couldn't let you go." Houses
Where we lived, already destroyed after us. Even
The echo of their fall is no more. I think how
*This time* is always in the singular
And *those days* in plural. And that I am one spearhead
Of an army of many, many days. Remember? "It is
The final conflict." The melody was beautiful
In those days. In this time.

My heart is now a wall, shadows of
Swaying branches make broader movements on it
Than in reality.
This is the nature of shadows,
The nature of the heart.

I'm longing again
For strangers' lit windows.
Perhaps a man, perhaps standing, perhaps
Before a mirror.
Or white snow falling inside,
A foreign king lying
On a woman who could have been
Mine.

A white Negress
On Ethiopian Street in Jerusalem
With the voice of a bold boy
Before it broke.

When I shall sit with her in a hot tub,
From the alleys I shall hear
Arguments about religion.

My heartbeat always beats me again
And nails me to the bed,
I return to the gestures of sleep I remember:
My knees are pulled up just as they buried
Me, or arms stretched as on a cross,
Or like a policeman directing traffic with one hand
Raised, the other beckoning.
Or a profile of a runner
On an old Grecian urn. One hand
On an upward angle and the body slanted.
Where am I running?

Put your face to the wind
For I do not know when again.
We have too little time left to forget.
We cannot rely on forgetting.
The wind pasted an old newspaper to the olive tree.
Put your face.

Once we stood together
As a symbol of a vanished kingdom:
Wild beasts, banners, and obsolete weapons
In one bundle, tied with a band of soothing words
In an ancient language.
A phrase from the prayerbook of history.
In your voice a tune still remained
Of Talmudic students.
"Do you love me?"
If we don't remain together, we won't remain at all.
Let alone live.

## ♦ WE DID IT ♦

We did it before the mirror
And in the light. We did it in the dark,
In the water, and in the tall grass.

We did it in honor of man
And in honor of animal and in honor of God.
But they would not hear about us,
They'd already seen it.

We did it with imagination and in color,
Mixing red hair with brown,
And with difficult exercises
Brimming with joy. We did it
Like seraphim and holy animals,
With the mystery of creation of the prophets.
We did it with six wings
And six legs, but the sky
Was hard above us
Like the summer ground below.

## MY FRIEND THE PHILOSOPHER
## AND HANUKAH

My friend uses a blackboard and chalk and rustling
Papers to explain himself. He
Is a philosopher. He uses the simple geometry
Of our love. Simple forms of a man
And a woman together. A closed square or triangle
Or an acute angle of hugging legs.
A circle and a matching one. Image of the world
Without the X of God. In my apartment hangs
My girl's lingerie to dry in the damp bathroom.
Tears dry faster.
My child lights Hanukah candles in Jerusalem,
A crown on his forehead with a paper candle.
I am awake and burn quietly: my love
Puts off the hour of my death, but prolongs
My agony, as in the time of the Inquisition
They put damp cotton on burning hearts.

These days I think of the wind in your hair
And of the years I came before you into the world
And of the eternity I shall exit to before you,

Of the bullets in the war that did not kill me
But my friends,
Who were better than me because they did not
Continue to live like me,

Of you standing in the summer naked before the stove
And how you bent over a book to see better
In the last light of day.

See, we had more than life,
Now we must weigh everything
With heavy dreams, and hurl
Haunting memories into what was the present.

# ✦ END OF ELUL* ✦

I'm tired of the summer. The smoke near the monastery of the silent nuns
Is all I have to say. This year, the winter
Will be late, when we shall be ready for it and shall not be.

I'm tired and curse the three famous religions
That won't let me sleep at night, with bells
And yells, pesty shofars and lamentations.

God, close your houses, let the world rest,
Why didn't You forsake me? The year is hesitant this year.
The summer goes on. If not for the tears
I amassed all those years, I would have dried with the thorns.

Great battles continue inside me in terrible silence,
Only the sighs, as of thousands of wrestlers, naked
And sweating. Not iron or stone, just flesh fighting like serpents.
Then they will fall off each other in passion,
And from the exhaustion, there will be clouds
And rain, when we shall be ready and shall not be.

*Roughly August–September, a month of serious contemplating in the Jewish calendar,
preceding the High Holy Days.

# Poems of Other Countries

### ✦ HOW MUCH TIME ✦

I remember the rain,
But I have forgotten things
The rain covered years ago.

My gaze is lifted
Like an airplane between control tower
And open spaces of abandonment and oblivion.

A foreign country covers
My face with its waters.
I am a sad general of streaming water.

Cambridge. Closed door of a friend's house:
How much time must pass
For such spiderwebs to take shape,
How much time?

My first days in New York,
We talked a lot about the death
Of God. We didn't talk,
We were just amazed that others
Discovered now what we had discovered
In the great desert
After bar mitzvah. Not
With thunder and lightning, not with a bang,
But in silence. And how
They managed to conceal his death
As one would conceal the death
Of a great and admired ruler leaving no heirs.

You will sail off. Your white hair will turn
The ship into a flagship.
You go to my city. I stay in yours.
A quiet exchange of places
In a game of friendship and of knowing death.

Recently, I saw you take some
Clothes to the cleaners,
So Jerusalem dust will be fresh on them.
Your arms embraced the large bundle
And I squeezed your empty coat sleeve
In farewell.

We are both of an age
Where they won't say orphan anymore
Of someone whose God has died.

# INDIAN SUMMER
## IN PRINCETON

Indian summer is Jewish summer
In your heavy eyes that always fall out
Because of their heaviness and because of the sadness
Of your face holding them.
Not because of dryness or the forgetfulness of fruit, but a falling
From heavy remembering. The ground keeps moving away from beneath
     us,
These leaves keep on falling.

It was Sunday, their Sabbath,
Time to sit down and ask ourselves
Whom we really love.
In the house lives
Someone different from the name on the gate.
A woman told me she doesn't love her life
And that some of the trees are sick like sick human beings.

But in my dream I look at dazzling Jerusalem.
Therefore, it is black now, like a picture
Overexposed.

### 1

It was not given me to linger at this lake,
As it was not given me to linger in many
Places where I wanted to linger. My wishes
Weary me more than my deeds. I didn't get used to
Any place. So, I wasn't weaned either.
To be weaned often—is to live. Death creates habit.

### 2

Today I saw traces
Of the last snow in a corner of a wall, in a passage between passages,
In the few days between winter's end and spring's beginning.
Old pain no longer hurts. The new hasn't yet begun to hurt.
And I am still among things
You can measure
With steps and beats of watch and heart.
A person wants to be a river in his youth.
But the breadth of my life scares me.
Rivers become very wide at their end.

### 3

In the other valley they shot and hunted. We were waiting for the thud
Of falling birds. A high lake slowly poured
Into a lower one. Give and take went on
In the other forest, a rustling discussion of all this.
To find gold on such a day: not the metal.
I breathe again lucid air, as a bell
Breathing lucid, precise time.

### 4

People tell you: "Come here in the summer,
You have to be here in the fall." Always
The season after you is the most beautiful.
You find yourself at windows

To decide, wondering where you are today
And where you'll wake up tomorrow. Places
Are passing by you. You don't choose. The wares
Will choose you: this one will buy me. I shall be his death.

### 5

In silent agreement, we arrived on different planes
In the unknown city where two rivers meet,
Like two diplomats coming to sign a treaty
Or to part. We are staying longer
In places where we wanted to stay a little.
We imagine this will stretch out our days. We imagine.

## TAKIS SINOPOLUS, GREEK POET

Takis Sinopolus has eyes the color of the sea.
He is a doctor outside and a poet inside. But
Where is the sea?
As he climbed up to the fourth floor, he breathed heavily
And swallowed two pills from a flat, secret box.

He too is saved every day from death.
When he looks at Rome from his balcony,
When he hears the beat of his heart,
He is a poet outside and a doctor inside.

But I know that even if he is not the sea,
He is at least Odysseus
Tied by his friends to the mast, at his own wish.
When their ears are plugged with wax, he hears.

Takis Sinopolus, your friends abandoned you long ago!
For a long time, you haven't reached your true homeland!
For a long time, you have remained tied to the mast. Listening.

Thus you stand before me with salty eyes on the fourth floor
And your hand, that should have touched
Your heart in sudden pain doesn't touch,
For you are tied to the mast.

You're not dead and I'm not dead:
We didn't keep what we promised each other
Twenty-five years ago. The moon
Still had a good or a bad face.
Kings passed through kingdoms that are no more.
Much breathing, long and short.
Smoke that didn't bring tears, for it was high.
Two or three wars. Words
We spoke then arrived here,
Waited in vain, and crumbled.

It seems that the music we heard then
Was the last calm music before
The great fear that hasn't stopped since,
A quarter of a century of fear and dread, not together.

What remained of that night
Of round water turning
Like a record of music.
Maybe like the life remaining after
One who departed:
Warm stove, bed somewhat warmer.

In a foreign country you must love
A student of history.
You lie with her in this grass
At the foot of these hills
And between groans and screams
She tells you what happened in the past.
"Love is a serious matter."
I never saw animals laughing.

Three times I came to Rome,
More and more entangled
In my problems. This time
We actually rolled into her
Like wrestlers entangled in each other,
I and my problems: beasts of prey,
Net and trident, sharp sword,
Early Christians, notched sword,
Stumbling in catacombs,
Emerging from the whistling Arch of Titus.
I didn't see any of those, I and my problems.
I could have stayed in Jerusalem.

Three times I came to Rome. This time
More honor, more pain,
More words in Italian—
Not just: Where is the train? How much?

And the gates are open to death all around.
Even the Porta San Sebastiano
I love.

### 1

Along the Hudson trade roads
And movements of armies that were. General Cornwallis
Went out to suppress a disturbance in the south
Which later became history.
He didn't know it, but he felt
With a flushed face at a bonfire
That I would pass many years later
To see the uselessness
Of such movements, of roads.

### 2

I walked with my friend along the river.
He collected colored glass the water
Washed onto the shore.
We walked on a path I shall never walk again,
On a day that will not return.
He told me of Guadalupe where he was,
Which I shall never see.
"Stop! Stop!" Too many distances.

### 3

Linked for eternity like a shore touching a river's water.
There is sand soaked in water and there is water
Dirty with sand.
But they are never one.

### 4

Only our voices walking by the water
Remained in this time. All other things,
Head, legs, dreams, nights,
Are already sold to the past, lent to the future,
Pawned to other places.

**5**

I can already answer if they ask me
About places in the foreign country. I already know
About them, I have interfered in things
That are none of my business.
The time has come to go. I ask if it makes sense
To make new connections or to discover
More places. I have postponed my flight
To see some green in the trees that were
Black in winter.
And I saw women whose cheekbones
And thighbones kept them upright
And tall. Beautiful and harsh women near soft gardens.
I saw all that, and now I must go.

Open closets are sad,
Drawers where your lingerie was,
Like a colorful season.
My prayers are sad. My money is sad,
And sad are my lies
Separating me from my sadness.

The branches of a pine tree sway
The wind back and forth.
What did we say then, in the afternoon hours.
The structure of the words was like a house of prayer,
Tall. An echo dome. What did we say
In the evening, your face between my legs
And my face between your legs, face to face
In a language far from all speech?

People with no future love people
With no past. They meet on a narrow strip.
The closer to their death
The more daring and brave they become.
Distances are packed in houses and gardens before
The passing window. When you travel, you hear,
Despite yourself, conversations of others.
You don't want to know anything about watches
That make you forget time. Despite yourself, you hear
And despite yourself, you live. A great rage
That was inside you turned into a soporific hum
Of a voyage. God leaves the country,
Of all times, now
When I live in it.
You can't change a thing.
You think of the voyage and its gear
And of precise fingers, making
Instruments and implements, airplanes from light metal
For a light farewell. You think about voyages
Not of escape and not of pleasure, but
Of others, as stones thinking
Of the compulsion of birds' voyages
They have inside them too.
Not envy and not longing, but my eyes
And my blood vessels and my hair and my travel gear
And the great heartbeat of trains in empty halls.

I drink the juice of fruit
I never saw growing or even
Squeezed.

Orphan girls on the road speaking Yiddish
In a hushed voice.
A baked mountain glowing in the distance.
A white tower on the Mount of Olives
Warning the Dead Sea not to come; like a finger.
The Old City came up to my window
Like a good horse that wants to drink and be stroked.

Inside there was screwing. She screamed chickens,
She-asses, lionesses.
Triangle hair met triangle hair,
Like two servants left in front of the door
When their masters meet in the red house.

"I haven't been so quiet in a long time." The garden
Penetrated through the back door.
Silence, cancer of silence.

The first rain reminds me
Of the rising summer dust.
The rain doesn't remember the rain of yesteryear.
A year is a trained beast with no memories.

Soon you will again wear your harnesses,
Beautiful and embroidered, to hold
Sheer stockings: you
Mare and harnesser in one body.

The white panic of soft flesh
In the place where the stocking stops being,
The panic of a sudden vision
Of ancient saints.

# Poems of Akhziv

Now in the din before the silence
I can tell you things
I didn't say in the silence before the din.
For they would have heard us and found our lair.

That we were just neighbors in the blowing wind,
Together in the old hot wind from the Land of Two Rivers.
And the last prophets of the kingdom of my veins
Prophesied into the firmament of your flesh.

And the weather was good for us and for our hearts
And the muscles of the sun hardened inside us in gold
In the Olympiad of emotions, above thousands of spectators.
So we know, so we remain, so there will be clouds again.

See, and we met in the sheltered place, in the corner
Where history began to rise, quiet
And safe from hasty feats.
And the voice began telling in the evening, at the children's bed.

And now it's too early for archaeology
And too late to repair what was done.
Summer will come, and the sound of the hard sandal's steps
Will drown in soft sand forever and ever.

They lied to us.
They told us: we shall die, wiped out in wars.
Ever since I can remember, they said: Our blood will be shed.
We ate and drank and didn't die tomorrow,
We squandered all we had saved, flowers for example, grass . . .

And in this spring I sometimes think,
What did you mean when you told me, "I'll give you
Only one night." Did you think
That *all the days of our lives* are nights, night,
Or did you say it out of the great dread.

They lied to us. I told my students everything
My teachers taught me. In great haste I told them,
So I would be free a bit and for myself in the end.
They lied to us:
The unshed blood
Screams louder
Than the shed.

Now to break
The words between us
Into sharp slivers:
"I can not ever live without you,"
And thrust them one by one
In the other's heart:
I
Can
Not
Live,
Ever,
Without you.
Live.
Not.

# FAMILY

I saw an old man. In his youth
He loved my mother-in-law. He could have been
The grandfather of my children. My mother-in-law
Is no longer my mother-in-law. My wife not my wife.
But my son, my son, my son.

The rabbi who joined us under the wedding canopy
Speaks a eulogy at the grave of a man
We didn't know together. In the telephone book
I saw my name by accident, after a long
Time. I don't live there. I'm not I.

My name and address like a verse from an old book.
But the name of my father and the name of my mother always
Find me out in all my weakness.

I utter sounds
Static on the radio. This is all I shall say.

To get entangled so in this beautiful world!
To change apartments four times in one year,
To be unneeded, unwashed,
With the ten martyrs of my soul
In the horrible torments of slow death.

But my son, my son. And my death, my death,
And wherever I go, I shall go with him.

Release her now.
Open your hand, a hand full of plenty
That will never again touch her thigh.
Release her. To what? Prepare. For what?
Explain to her claims and clouds.
A fortune-teller she was to you, telling future and past,
And a tamer of holy animals,
A secrets-cracker
Of the holy labor of lovemaking by the angels of sex,
God's dog, His wrath and His bitch.

In her slumber she prepares, in her window
The gaze of the two is displayed like a lamp, forever.
That was and that will not be, her walk, her curly hair,
Wild, barefoot childhood. A daughter of the groves. Release
Her. You yourself enter now the grove
As those Four Sages. Alone. Release her. Now
You became another, you cannot be returned.

Rabbi Nakhman of Bratslav
Did strange feats
In Istanbul. Byzantine feats
In dim light. A sighing mosaic
In a thousand husky colors.

Rabbi Nakhman did and came to the Land of Israel
And didn't stay.
I do them in Jerusalem.
Silence is best.

He had a long beard, by which
His Hasidim knew where the wind was blowing.
Seeds of thorns flew in the spring,
Seeds of dandelion with little white parachutes.

He had sidelocks
By which God pulled him out of all evil.
I don't.

# ✦ TOURIST ✦

She showed me her hair turning
To the four winds of her coming.
I showed her some ways of my folding life
And the trick and the lock.
She asked me for my street and my house
And I laughed aloud.
She showed me this long night
And the inside of her thirty years.
I showed her the place of the tefillin
I once put on.

I brought her proverbs and verses and colored sand from Eylat
And the giving of the Torah and the manna of my death and all the
    miracles
That did not heal in me.

She presented to me the stages
Of joy and the return of her childhood.
I revealed to her that King David is not buried in his grave,
That I do not live in my life.
She believed me.

When I was brooding, she ate.
The map of the city was spread on the table:
One of her palms on Katamon,
My palm on hers.
The mug covered the Old City.
Ashes dropped on the King David Hotel.
The pain of our forefathers shielded us.
Ancient weeping undid our groins.

## 1

Broken near the sea,
My head a broken tin.
Sea water fills it
And seeps out.

Broken near the sea.
Elegy, song of my nest,
Foam on lips of the reefs.
Rabies has the sea,
Seabies it has,
More rabid than a dog
More sea than any sea.

Broken near the sea
Song of my nest, elegy.

## 2

The wheels of ancient millstones were parted
And put on display, the lower stone, and the upper stone,
In two ends of the village.
Out of deep longing
They continue to grind between them
The time of lovers.

Naked people in the sand talk about
Political problems. Ridiculous!
In the distance, small heaps of clothes.
Birds shriek from an island. Pink buttocks
And muscles like sleeping fish. Ridiculous
Even to ask "what time is it"
When you're naked. A strip of white skin on your left wrist.
Better a dialogue:

"Dia," she said. "Logue," he said,
Dia, dia, dia, logue, logue.

Our friend hid a typewriter
In a broom bush. Camouflaged by branches.
Tick, tock, dia, dia, dia, logue.

### 3

All night long you lay awake on your back.
There was a different wind
And there was a wind that was like you.
The moonlight
Covered the wall
With another thatch.
"The key is under the stone at the gate."
In the morning we shall see the contour of your body
Marked with cigarette butts
On the floor.

### 4

Your green eyes were
Blue for my brown eyes
After this night.

Wrinkles appeared on the sheet;
Not of old age.

### 5

In midsummer, over the water
Near Akhziv, it suddenly came to me
"Rock of Ages let our song," a melody of snow
And Hanukah.

In my childhood I was in the places where the Maccabees
Fought in snow and in the forests. But even then
The voices were prepared to leap
Into my time now. Suddenly,

Over the water, on my back, it came to me:
Rock of Ages. Sheltering tower. Praise.

### 6

Around the dead word "we loved,"
Covered with seaweed in the sand,
Many onlookers crowded.

Till night we heard the testimonies
Of waves coming one by one,
Of how it happened.

### 7

He who amasses waves amasses eyes,
He who amasses torments amasses salt,
He who amasses sleep amasses worms,
He who amasses sadness sings at night, amasses
Shells, amasses sand, sand, everything.

That means—to go on living.
What is our life: a few centimeters
Of madness and soft flesh
Between the hard skeleton inside
And the hard air outside.

### 8

My friend saw horses bathing
In the sea at Acre. He saw, and I feel
Them galloping. What did we seek
In the sand on the third day and the fourth day,
What did we seek?
With a light puff I blew out your right ear.
With a light puff I blew out your left ear.
With light puffs in your two ears
I lit your lust. A great
Invasion into us
Began. Our throbbing, entangled
Bodies witnessed the immensity of the struggle. In vain.

### 9

Tie your weeping in a chain
And be inside with me.

In the half ruined house
Light lives alone.
From the dark, they make delicate silver work
For the last supper.

The mouth of a fish, my mouth
And the mouth of a fish, your nipple
Joined in the night.
Then, the moon night was
Whiter than Yom Kippur.
Your weeping tore the chain.
Fled far away.

### 10

In the sand we were a two-headed Cerberus
Baring our teeth. At noon
Your one leg was in the east, the other in the west,
And I in the middle, leaning on my forelegs,
Looking suspiciously to the sides, roaring terribly
So they wouldn't rob me of my prey.

Who are you?
A little Jewish boy from the Diaspora,
A *yarmulke* on his head. From there. From that time.

At night we are together with no
Heavy memory, no sticky feelings. Just
Ingathering of muscles and their dispersion.

Far away from here, in another continent of time,
You can clearly see the dead rabbis of my childhood,
Holding high above their heads
The tombstones. Their souls bound in the bond of my life.
My God, my God,
Why did You not forsake me!?

With a daring Columbus gaze
I look through towels hung
At a window. The sun is setting
Into a red dress.
Four boats passed from evening
To evening behind a kerchief.
Salt in the little salt shaker on the table
And outside, all the salt in the world.


Seven creased underpants
Around your bed, for the seven
Days we were here. Like
Seven withering roses
In seven colors

One-piece bathing suit:
Many voices of the crowd.
Somersault of games.
Applause of my hands on your body,
Stormy applause.


Dry measure and wet
Measure in hard longing
Destroy each other.


Crossroads of veins.
Blue pretends to be pink.
In your ankle I shall live.
My member rises with great solemnity
As if to attention.


I shall leave you at the sea
Until your red hair turns green,
Until my black briefcase is covered with green moss
Like a ship sunk long ago.
I shall draw screams from inside you,

Reparations for all the silence I bled.
Vengeance.
God.


### 13

Two-piece bathing suit.
Two small pieces
Bathing suit
Bathing
Suit.
Sea.


### 14

Akhziv, flowing juices,
Flowing gold,
Naked butt,
But, but.

Soon the abandoned village
Will be abandoned again
By us. But you,
Brown hair, white skin,
Green eyes; but here,
In Akhziv, all the red
Breaks out of you,
Reveals: you are one
Of the thirty-six hidden red saints.
Moss between your thighs,
Red,
Like Esau.


### 15

The Ladders of Tyre, the ladders of lust,
The ladders to the roof of Eli's house. Girls
Descend and ascend, carrying mattresses and lines,
Long hair and underwear to be dried. Shouts
Of laundry. The dampness of laughter won't dry.
Girls ascend and descend the ladder.

You can see her soul:
Black and made of thin net.
You can see her pink underwear,
With delicate lace. You can see her,
See her, see her.

16

Wind, what a waste of wind
You are. To shift sand to sand,
Me to you, smell to smell.
Wind, what a waste!

Clouds, what a waste of clouds,
Not to rain, just to change
The colors of the Western Galilee a bit
For us.
My life, what a waste of life
It is. Only for these days. Here.

17

I learned
To treat your cunt
Like a face.
I talk her ancient tongue.
She is wrinkled, made of matter more ancient
Than all the generations of memory, written in the book.

She treats us
Like distant great-grandchildren,
Playing.

18

The last night at the window,
Outside and inside. Seven o'clock,
Nine, ten. The eleventh hour:
Moonlight
Turned our bodies into scalpels,
Hard and glittering in evil.
Another hour, one o'clock, two, three,

Five: in the first light of dawn
Your body appears trapped in the net
Of its veins, like a sheet
That fell down at night and was caught
In the branches of a dead tree
In front of the window.

19

In the abandoned house
Live Tamarisk Dwarf, Mint
And Sage. We shall visit them
After noon, sit with them,
Rustle with them and exude a fragrant odor.


On your loins a ruddy line,
Memory of an elastic band,
Like a line in the sand disappears with a wave,
And we shall know:
Our days here are ripe.

20

How is it to be woman?
How is it to feel
Emptiness between your legs and curiosity
In a skirt, in the summer, in the wind,
And boldness in your buttocks.


A man has to live with the strange bag
Between his legs. "Where would you want
It to be?" asked the tailor, measuring my pants
And didn't smile.


How is it a whole voice that won't break?
How is it to get dressed and undressed
Gliding and sliding and caressing,
Like wearing olive oil,
To anoint your body with soft cloth,
Something silky, murmuring nothings of pink or blue?

A man dresses with coarse movements of
Buckling and hard tearing,
Angles, bones, and punching the air.
And the wind is entangled in his whiskers.

How is it to feel woman?
Your body dreams you.
How is it to love me?
The vestiges of a woman in my male body
And the male signs in your body
Herald the hell
Waiting for us
And our mutual death.

## 21

If the longings begin
Among these houses near this sea,
We shall be far away.

The mourning women in my heart
Began too early, while I'm still here,
To lament and tear my blood and the sand of the sea
And its weeds; and to bang their fist on the rock,
On the sand, on your breasts.

The sea retreated from my face.
My face is like the floor of the sea: dry
With crevices and rocks and harsh winds.
Thus I am mature
And the memories of the soft green sea still on my face.

## 22

After these days, I don't know much
About you. The palm tree stayed bent to the east
Even without a west wind. A white boat
Passes along the shore, tough
And clear as God's finger. The will
I'm writing in Akhziv, in the sand,
Is different from the will I wrote in Jerusalem.

The voices of children buried in the layers
Of the mound reach us in this century
At this hour of noon. They did not
Stop playing.

Never shall the white, weatherbeaten board
Be again in the ship, never will a rock be made
From the crushed gravel. This tears
My soul, as it was torn by the Prophets; in a rip
Of sharp pain a man becomes a prophet.
This is the landscape for forgetting and prophecy.
From now on, we shall seek other windows with other
Images. We shall wander from window to window, from vault to vault.

The anchor of the abandoned ship will soon
Decorate houses and yards. Our heart will be just an amulet
Hanging inside dreams and blood.

# The Travels of Benjamin the Last, of Tudela

✦ THE TRAVELS OF BENJAMIN ✦
THE LAST, OF TUDELA

You ate and drank your fill. You arrived here
In your twelfth year, in the world's
Thirties, your pants were knee-high, tassels
Hanging down the four wings of your undergarment, sticky
Between your legs, in this hot land. Your skin
Still smooth, unprotected by hair. Your brown, round eyes,
On the scale of ripe cherries, will learn oranges.
Celibate wholeness. Citrus color. Watches
Were set by your round heartbeats. Railroad tracks,
By the perseverance of a child's legs.

And calmly, like a doctor, or a mother,
The days bent over me, whispering among themselves,
While the grass lay flattened by its bitter wind,
On hillsides I shall never tread again.
The moon, the stars, the ancient acts of grown-ups
Were placed on a high shelf, my arms won't reach.
I stood in vain at the forbidden bookcase. Yet even then
I was marked for destruction, as an orange
Marked for peeling, as chocolate, as a hand grenade
For blowing up and death.
Intentions held me tight in their hand. My sky was
The inside of the soft holding palm, and outside:
Rough skin, hard stars, bulging veins,
Air lines, black hair, shell trajectories
Through dead matter or through wailing creatures,
In black or with gleaming tracers.

And before I was a real person, lingering here,
My heart bore on its shoulders a sadness not my own.
Alien ideas entered, restrained, slowly
Moving, gurgling deeply, like a train
Into a hollow, listening station.

You ate and drank and blessed,
Alone and in tandem and alone,
In the room of copulation after the wedding canopy, while outside
Bearded witnesses attended to the voices of love,
The coos, the sighs, the screams—mine and hers—
In the room of copulation. And the door was blocked with wedding gifts
Like the death gifts in the tombs of Egyptian kings.
The stone lions on the bridges of my native city protected us,
Along with the stone lions of the old house in Jerusalem.

You didn't eat or drink your fill. You spoke big words
With your small mouth. Your heart will never learn to
Estimate distances. The most distant is the closest tree, the edge
Of the sidewalk, the face of your beloved. Like a blind man,
Your blind heart hits an obstacle with its stick, to this day
It hits and gropes and doesn't advance. Hits, will hit. Loneliness
Is a time for conjugating actions. Hits, will hit. Time
Is smell. The smell of 1929, for instance, when the sadness blessed you
As its first fruit *that we lived to see*. You didn't know
You were its first fruit.

You were raised in a kindergarten by the Montessori method.
They taught you to love doing things with your own hands. They
    prepared you
For loneliness. You spilled your seed in vain. Nightly happenings,
Daily events. "I shall tell your father." Hollow, echoing
Rosh Hashana halls, white machines of Yom Kippur
In bright metal, cogs of prayers, a conveyor belt of bows,
Scary buzzing. You sinned, you transgressed
In a dark womb shaped like a synagogue dome,
The round, ancient prayer cave. The gaping Holy Ark dazzled you
With a third-degree interrogation. Do you confess? Confess?
*I confess to You* in the morning, when the sun is outside.

Name? You surrender? You sinned, you waxed fat, you're alive?
How are you? ("You love me?"). You remembered, you forgot.

Oh, Montessori, Montessori, the white-haired woman,
The first dead I loved. "Child, child!"—to this day I turn around
When I hear it in the street behind me.

Slowly, with excruciating pain, "I" turned into "he," after
Resting a while in "you." "She" to "they." The operation was performed
With eyes open, perhaps just locally anesthetized with ice
Or love potion. Behind you too, they will shout: Dreamer! Dreamer!
You won't be able to. What is your name now? Not even
One name did I carry in vain. Names are good for children.
A grown-up keeps a distance from his name. He's left
Just with the family name. Then: father, teacher, uncle, Mister, Oh Mister,
Hey, you there! (Do you love me?—that's different,
More than a name), then numbers, then perhaps:
He, he left, they will return, they, hey! Hey!
The forest of names is naked, the kindergarten too.
It shed the leaves of its trees, it's black and will die.

And on the Sabbath eve they sewed my handkerchief
To the corner of my pants pocket, not to carry it on the Holy Sabbath,
Not to sin. And on holidays, priests blessed me
From the white caves of their prayer shawls with twisted
Fingers of epileptics. I looked at them
But God did not thunder: since then, His thunder has kept
Receding and has turned into a great silence. I looked at them
But my eyes did not go blind: since then my eyes keep
Opening from year to year evermore, till no sleep,
Till pain, till no eyelids, no clouds, no year.
Death is not sleep but your eyes gaping, your whole body
Gapes open with your eyes, for lack of room in the narrow world.

Angels appeared as Torah Scrolls in velvet dresses and white
Silk slips, with crowns and silver bells, angels
Hovered around me, sniffed my heart and called Ah Ah
To each other with a grown-up's smile. "I shall tell your father."
And to this day, thirty-three years later, my father's

Blessing remained in my hair, though it grew wild as the Negev
Sticky with blood and dust of loess, and though I cut and trimmed it
To a war brush and a French city pompadour, sad
and sticking to my forehead. Still,
The blessing remained in the hair of my blessed pate.

You came in through Haifa. The port was new, the boy was new.
You lay on your belly, not to kiss the holy ground,
But because of the shootings of 1936. British soldiers
Wearing the cork hats of a vast empire,
Messengers of a disintegrating kingdom, opened the gate to
The new kingdom of your life. "Your name?" Soldiers
Opened the gate with tattooed arms: a dragon, a woman's
Breasts and thighs, a knife, a winding ancient serpent,
A big rose, a girl's behind. Since then, tattoos
And their images have sunk into you, though invisible from
Outside. The writing sinks, a permanent etching and pain,
Into your soul, it too a parchment writing, scrolled
Like a mezuzah along your inside body.
You became a collector of pains in the tradition of this land.
*"Eli, Eli, lama?"* Why have You forsaken me. *Eli, Eli,* my God, my God.
    Then too
They had to call Him twice. The second call
As a question, in first doubt: *Eli?* My God?

I haven't said the last word yet. I haven't yet
Eaten, but I had my fill. My coughing is not
From smoke or illness, but a condensed,
Time-saving form of questions.
All that was as if it never was, and all the rest
I do not know. Perhaps it is written in the difficult books on the shelf,
In the concordances of pain and the dictionaries of joy,
In the encyclopedias with pages stuck together like eyes that will not
Release their dream at dawn, in the awesome correspondence
Between Marx-and-Engels, I-she, God-he,
In the book of Job, in the difficult words. Verses
That are deep cuts in my flesh. Long wounds,
Red from lashes, wounds filled with white salt, like the meat
My mother salted and made kosher, not to show blood but

Pink salt sated with blood, but pain
That is caustic knowledge, kosher and pure.
The rest—unknown, alienation in the dark. Like the brothers in Egypt
We shall wait, kneeling in the dark of our knees, hiding our meek
Faces, till the world cannot restrain itself anymore
And weeps and cries: I am your brother Joseph! I am the world!

When the war broke out, I passed by the belly of your mother
Where you already sat curled up, as at night with me.
The rhythm of the orchard pumps and of the shooting was our rhythm.
It starts! Light and pain, iron and dust and stones.
Stones and flesh and iron in changing combinations
Of materials. Give the materials their due! Dust, dust,
From man you came and to man you shall return. It starts!
My blood flows in many colors and pretends to be red
When it bursts out of my body. My beloved's navel too
Is an eye to see the end. The end and the beginning in her body.
Two creases in her right buttock, one crease in the left,
Glimmering glasses at the skin of a white belly, an eyebrow
Concave with the eye's scream, soft black silk on
Taut skin of thick thighs. A clear, protruding shoulder,
Divided with a strap of black, precise cloth.
Shoulder to shoulder, flesh to flesh, dust to dust.

As a legend and a child, to love and back, world and ear,
Time in a conch's smile, you will love and open up:
The home is for the night, the earth for the dead and the rain
On the morning after the giving of the sun. Spring evoked in us
Green speech, the summer bet that we would arrive first,
And love broke out of us, all of a sudden, from the whole body,
Like sweat, in the fear of our lives, in the run of our lives, in a game.
And children grew and matured, for the water level rises
Incessantly in the awesome flood, and all their growing is
Because of the rising flood, not to drown.
And still, with fingers stained by the moon, as a teacher's with chalk,
God strokes our head, the joints of His hands are
Songs and angels! And His elbows! And the face
Of the woman, already turned to another matter. A profile in the window.

The veins in my legs protrude, for my legs ruminate
A lot, their walking is rumination. The empty wasteland
Of my feelings: the wild beasts have abandoned it when I created
And drained and made my life settled culture; now they returned.
Long lines of books, restful rooms and corridors.
My body is built for good resonance, like a concert hall,
The sound of weeping and screams will not pass. The walls absorb,
Airtight, the waves of memories return. And above me, on the ceiling,
Childhood objects, soft words, women's dresses, father's prayer shawl,
Half bodies, big woolly toys, clouds,
Chunks of Good-Night, heavy hair: to strengthen the resonance in me.

Dust, dust, my body, installation of my halflife.
Still daring scaffolds of hopes, ladders trembling over
The unfinished from the outside, even the head is but
The lowest of the stories that were planned.
My eyes, one alert and interested, the other indifferent
And distant, as if perceiving everything from the inside, and my hands
Pulling sheets over the dead and the living. Finished and sealed.
My shaving face, the face of a white-foamed clown, the only foam
Not of rage. My face, something between a mad bull
And a nomadic bird that lost the direction of its migration
And is left behind the flock, but can see slow and good things
Before its death in the sea.
Even then, and since then always, I encountered
The stagehands of my life, the movers of walls
And furniture and people, raising and lowering
New illusions of new houses, diverse landscapes, distances
In perspective, not real distances, closeness
But not real closeness. All of them, all,
My friends and my foes, are the stage directors and stagehands,
Electricians illuminating in a different light, moving away
Or closer, changing and changers, hanging and hung.

All his life, my father tried to make me into a man
With a hard face like Kosygin or Brezhnev,
Like generals and admirals, stockbrokers and administrators.
All those are the imaginary fathers I appointed
Instead of my father, in the soft land of the seven kinds of fruit

(Not just two, male and female, but seven kinds beyond us,
More desirous, harder and deadlier than ours).
I have to screw a hero's expression onto my face
Like a bulb screwed well into the hard threads of its socket.
All his life, my father tried to make me into
A man, but I always slide back
Into the softness of thighs and yearnings to bless
*That he made me in his will.* And his will is woman.
My father was afraid to bless in vain.
To bless the Creator of fruit and not eat the apple.
To bless without loving. To love not to the fill.
I ate but not to the fill and didn't bless.
My life spread out and separated:
In my childhood, there were still stories of kings and ghosts
And blacksmiths, now glass domes and shining space ships
And glimmering silences with no hope.
My hands stretched out to a past not mine and a future
Not mine: hard to love, hard to lock an embrace
With such hands.
As a butcher hones his knives on one another
I hone a heart on a heart inside me. The hearts
Grow sharper and dwindle, but the movement of my soul
Always remains the sharpener, and my voice will be lost in metal clang.

And on Yom Kippur you ran in sneakers.
And at *Holy, Holy, Holy* you leaped high,
Higher than everybody, almost to the angels of the ceiling,
And on Simhat Torah you circled the Torah Scroll
Seven times seven, and arrived breathless.
Like a weightlifter you pushed up
The Torah Scroll, raising it with two trembling arms,
So they all see the writing and the strength of your hands.

At *kneeling and bowing* you fell to the floor
As for a great leap into the rest of your life.
And on Yom Kippur you launched a boxing match
Against yourself: *We sinned, we betrayed,*
With heavy fists and no gloves,

Nervous featherweight against heavy, sad weight
Then surrendering. The prayers ran from the corner of your mouth
In a thin red stream. Between the circles, they wiped
The sweat of your brow with your prayer shawl.

The prayers you prayed in your childhood
Now return and fall from above
Like bullets that didn't hit and return
To the earth after a long time,
Nobody pays attention, no harm done.
When you lie with your love
They return. "I love you," "You
Are mine," I confess to you. "And you love"
God your Lord. "With all my being," you must get excited
And not sin and be silent, amen. Silence.
Calling *Shema, listen,* in bed. In bed
Without calling *listen.* The redoubled cave
Of a bed. *Shema. Shema.*
Listen now once more, my dear,
Without *Shema.* Without you.

Not God's finger but His ten fingers
Choke me. "I won't let you
Let me leave you." This too
Is one of the interpretations of death.
You forget yourself as you were.
Do not accuse the chief butler of forgetting
Joseph's dreams! Hands still sticky
With candle wax forgot the holiday of Hanukah.
The creased masks of my face forgot
The joy of Purim. The body, ascetic
On Yom Kippur, forgot the High Priest,
Beautiful like you, on this night, forgot the hymn
In his praise: A priest's countenance like the sun, like a diamond,
Like a topaz, a priest's countenance. And her body too
Is Urim and Tumim, your nipples, your eye,
Your nostrils, your mole, your navel, my mouth, your mouth,
All those shone for me like the High Priest's breastplate,

Told me and prophesied my deeds. I flee
Before your body
Prophesies the future, I flee.

Sometimes I want to return
To all I had, as in a museum,
When you return not in the order
Of the periods, but in reverse, against the arrows,
To seek the beloved woman.
Where is she? The Egyptian room,
The Far East, the Twentieth Century, Cave
Art, everything mixed up, and the worried
Guards call to you:
This is against the periods! Not there!
Here is the Exit. You won't learn from this,
You know you won't. You seek, you forget.
As when you hear the march of a military band
In the street, and you remain where you stood and hear
It get farther away. Little by little, its sounds
Disappear: first the little bells, then
The big trumpets grow silent,
Then even the oboes sink in the distance,
Then even the sharp flutes, even
The little drums, but for a long time
The kettle drums still remain,
The skeleton of the tune, a heartbeat, until
Even those. *And they were silent forever. Amen.*

On Rosh Hashana you issue the order
To the horn blower: *Tekiyah, Teruah, Shevarim!*
Blow! Blast! Broken notes! Rage, Great Rage, Great Blow!
Fire! At every target before your eyes, fire!
Cease. Stop. Sit down. Today the world's pregnant moment!
World end! Today all creatures ever are on trial!
Synagogues are fortresses aimed at Jerusalem,
The loopholes of their windows at the Holy East.

The *shofar* forgot my lips,
The words forgot my mouth,

The sweat evaporated from my skin,
The blood gelled and dropped off,
The pointing hand forgot my hand,
The blessing vanished from the hair of my head,
The radio still warm,
The bed got cold before.
The seam between day and night
Came undone, you might slip out
Of your life and disappear unnoticed.
Sometimes, you need a few days
To overcome one single night.
History is a eunuch,
Looking for mine too
To castrate, cut with paper sheets
Sharper than any knife, to crush,
To block my mouth forever
With whatever she cut,
As a desecration of the war dead,
So I sing only an impotent chirp,
So I learn many languages
And not one tongue of my own,
So I am scattered and dispersed,
Not a Tower of Babel rising to heaven.

Not to understand is my happiness,
To be like imbecile angels,
Eunuchs soothing with their song.

The time has come to play
With technical toys, machines and their parts,
Mechanical toys, automatic,
Springing, self-propelling in their sleep,
Wheels that roll and buttons that start,
All that moves and jumps and leaps and emits
Pleasant sounds, slaves and servant girls,
A he-instrument and a she-instrument,
A chest of mistress and a chest of drawers,
Eunuchs and eunuchs of eunuchs.
My life is spiced with heavy lies

The longer I live, the art of forgery
Grows in me, becomes
More authentic. Artificial flowers
Look more and more natural
And plants look factory-made.
Who, after all, can distinguish
Between an authentic bill and a counterfeit?
Even the watermarks
Embossed in me
Can be forged: my heart.
My unconscious has grown used to light
Like bacteria adapting with time
To a new disinfectant.
A new underground organized,
The low under the lowest.

Forty-two years of light and forty-two
Years of night. Gorging and guzzling,
Like the late Roman emperors
In the used history books, scribbles of a crazy drawing
And writing on the wall in a toilet,
Annals of heroism and conquest and decline
And life in vain and death in vain.
Revolutions and revolts, and the suppression of revolts
During a banquet. In a sheer nightgown,
Fluttering, you rose in revolt against me, hair
Streaming like a banner above and hair standing on end below.
Blast, great blast. Broken bottle
And blast. Suppression of the revolt with straps
Of a woman's garters, choking with sheer stockings,
Stoning with sharp heels of party shoes.
Circus-battles of one armed with a broken bottle neck
Against a net of delicate panties, shoes
Against treacherous lace, tongue against hayfork,
Half a fish against half a woman. Straps and buttons,
Tangles of bras, trimmed with sprigs, against buckles
And an army belt. Blast and suppression of blast.
Shouts of soccer from the nearby field,
And I was lying on top of you, heavy and quiet

Like weights, so that wind and time could not
Fly you away like paper or hours.


"Where do you feel your soul inside you?"
Between my mouth-hole and my asshole it stretches,
A white thread, not a transparent breath,
Crouching in some corner between two bones,
In pain.
When it has its fill, it disappears like a cat.
I belong to the last generation of
Those who know body and soul separately.
"What do you plan to do tomorrow?"
I cannot wean myself from myself. I was weaned
From smoking and drinking and from the God of my fathers,
I was weaned from all that may hasten my end.


The smell of a new bicycle I got as a gift
In childhood is still in my nostrils, the blood
Not yet dried and I already want calm, other gods,
The god of order, as on the Seder night: the four
Questions and the ready answer, reward and punishment,
Ten plagues, four Matriarchs, egg, arm, bitter herb,
It's all ordered, Had Gadya, the famous soup, the safe
Matzo dumplings, nine months of pregnancy, forty
Blows on the sea. And the heart trembles a bit
Like the door for the Prophet Elijah,
Neither open nor closed. "And it was at midnight." Now
The children are put to bed. In their sleep
They still hear the sounds of grinding
Jaws: the world feasts on a great feast.
The sound of swallowing is the voice of history,
Hiccups and belches and bone grinding are the voices of history,
Bowel movements are her movements. Digestion. Digested,
Everything begins to resemble everything else:
Brother and sister, man and his dog, good man and evil man,
Flower and cloud, shepherd and lamb, ruler and ruled, all of them,
Descending to similarity. My experimental life too descends.
Everything descends into terrible similarity. Everything the fruit of the
    guts.

Now turn around, my dear. Let everyone see the hollow
That goes down her back and deepens between her buttocks. Who
Can say where those start and where
The thighs end. Here are the bold supports
Of the pelvis, the pillars of the legs,
And the curls decorating the Hellenistic gate
Above the groin. The Gothic arch aspiring
To the heart and a red Byzantine candle between
Her legs. Bend over into a typical Moorish style,
Crusader influence is marked in the hard cheekbones,
The prominent chin. She touches the ground with two palms
Without bending her knees, she touches
The ground I didn't kiss when I was brought
To the land in my childhood. All of you, come back and visit
Our land, visit my tears and the east wind,
Which is the true Western Wall. It is made
Of big windstones and the weeping is the weeping of the wind
And the papers swirling in the air are supplication notes
I stuck in the cracks. Visit our land. On a clear day,
If the visibility is good, you can
See the great miracle of my child
Holding me in his arms while he is four
And I am forty-four.
And here is the zoo of the great beloved,
Acres of love. Hairy animals breathing
In the cages of a panty net, feathers and brown
Hair, red fish in green eyes,
Hearts isolated beyond bars of ribs
Jump like monkeys, hairy fish and serpents
In the form of a plump round thigh.
And a body, ardent and shining red, covered
With a wet raincoat. That's soothing.

This earth talks only if they hit
It, if hail and rain and bombs hit it,
Like Balaam's ass that talked only after
Its master hit it hard. I'm talking,
I'm talking: I was hit, blast, great blast.
Sit down. Today is apocalypse.

I want to bet with Job
How God and Satan will behave.
Who will curse man first.
Like the redness of sunset in Job's mouth,
They hit him and his last word sinks
In red into his last face.
I left him like that in the bustling station
In the clamor, among the voices on the loudspeaker.
"Damn it, Job. Cursed be the day
You were born in My image. Your mother's cunt, Job."
God cursed, God blessed. Job won.
And I have to commit suicide with the toy gun
Of my little son.

My son blossoms sadly.
He blossoms in the spring without me,
He will ripen in the sadness-of-my-not-being-with-him.
I saw a cat playing with her kittens,
I shall not teach my son war,
I shall not teach him at all. I shall not be.
He pours sand into a small bucket.
He makes a cake.
I pour sand into my body.
The cake crumbles. My body.

I ate and drank my fill. As soon as one came
Another came, as soon as one spoke another spoke.
Birthdays came to me on the run,
Hastily. A quiet moment on a floating board.
My forty-third birthday. The anniversary
Of your wedding with yourself and with no chance for divorce.
Separate beds of dream and day,
Of your will and your love.
I live outside my mother's teaching and in countries
That are not my father's ethic. The walls of my house
Were constructed by builders not prophets, and on the portico
I discovered the year of my birth carved in stone.
("What did the house achieve and what did I!")
In the afternoon, I take a quiet stroll

Among the exterritorial wounds of
My life: a lighted window, behind it perhaps you undress
Now. A street where we were. A black door
Over there. A garden next to it. A gate through which. A dress
Like your dress on a body not yours. A mouth singing like
A word almost. All those are external wounds in a great
Garden of wounds.

I wear colorful clothes,
I am a colorful male bird.
Too late I have discovered that this is the order of nature.
The male preens. Red shirt, green
Coat. Don't catch me at it, my son!
Don't laugh. You don't see me. I am part
Of the wall. My shirt collar darkens.
A dark line under my eyes. Dark coffee grounds
And dark mourning in my fingernails. Don't catch me
At it, my son. With my hands, smelling of tobacco
And foreign perfume, I knead your dreams
In the future, I prepare your subconscious.
My child's first memory is the day
I left his home, my home. His memories
Are hard as diamonds in a watch that hasn't stopped
Since then. When the woman asks him on his first night
Of love, as they lie naked on their backs,
He will tell her: "The first time my father left."

And my childhood of blessed memory. I filled my share
Of revolt, I fulfilled the requirement of a rebellious son,
I contributed my part in the war of generations and the unruliness
Of adolescence. Hence, I had little time left
For rest and satiation. This
Is the whole person. And blessed be my childhood's memory.
My insomnia turned me into a nightwatchman
With no special task of what to watch.
"Happy birthday to you, happy birthday to you," the understanding
Of sixty and the valor of eighty, the wisdom of seventy,
And the gray hair of ninety, knowledge and death,
Came to me all at once. The memory of my childhood. Blessed.

I returned home, a jungle hunter of feelings.
On my walls, horns and wings and heads,
Stuffed feelings all over.
I sit and watch them serenely, don't
Catch me at it, my son. Even my laughter shows
That I cannot laugh anymore, and the mirror has known
For a long time that I am its reflection,
Don't catch me at it, my son, your eyes are darker than mine,
Perhaps you are already sadder than I.
My heavy body shakes its hearts as the hand of a gambler
Shakes the dice before he throws them on the table.
This is the motion of my body, this is its game, this is my destiny.

Bialik, a bald knight among olive trees,
Didn't write poems in the Land of Israel, for he kissed
The ground and brushed away flies and mosquitoes with his
Writing hands and wiped the sweat off his singing head
And in the hot wind he covered his head with a kerchief from the
    Diaspora.

Richard, his lion heart peeps out and pokes a long tongue
Between his ribs. He too was brought
In a traveling circus to the Holy Land. He, a lion heart,
And I, a kicking jackass heart.
All of us in a deadly somersault, painted clowns,
Smeared with white blood, feathers and armor, swallowing
Swords and honed crosses, acrobats
With bells. Oh, Sultan, *salto mortale*, the plate of justice
Jingles empty, fire-eaters and sprinklers
Of baptismal water, danseuses with male sex organs.
The King David Hotel floats in the air,
Its residents asked for milk, and got dynamite in jugs:
Destroy, destroy, blood and fire in candy stands,
You can also get fresh blood, foaming in juice extractors
Of heroism, twisted war dead, with stiff limbs
Like bagels strung on a thread.

Yehuda Halevi is bound in his books, caught in the webs
Of his longing, spun by himself. He was held as hostage,

A poet died in Alexandria. I don't remember
His death, as I don't remember my death,
But I do remember Alexandria: the street of the sisters,
Sixty-six. General Shmuel Hanagid on his horse,
As burned and black as the trunks of charred olive trees,
Riding around the round Ethiopian church,
So he imagined the Temple.
Napoleon, hand on his heart, compares the beat
Of his heart to the beat of his cannons.
And a woman's panties, small and triangular, on a line
On a roof in Jerusalem—signaling to the tired veteran
Sailor from Tudela, Benjamin the Last.

I lived for two months in the quiet of Abu Tor,
I lived for two weeks in the Valley of the Son of Hinnom,
In a house they destroyed after me, and in another house
Where an additional story was built, and in a house
Whose walls were buttressed as they never
Buttressed me. House takes precedence over man.
Sit seven days of mourning now, get used to sitting low
Where all life will look like towers to you.
Eulogy disperses in the city cursed by winds, ancient
Jerusalem rustles with the silence of evil gold. The magic
Of yearning. The air of valleys flogged by olive branches
To new wars, black olives, hard
As a whip, no hope between my eyes,
No hope between my legs in the redoubling
Of the caps of my lust. Even the chapter of my bar mitzvah
Was double, *inseminate-leper*, telling
Of skin diseases, shining in wounded colors, in dying red
And in the yellow of Sodom-sulfur of pus.
Mumbling of the millennialists, numerologies of torture,
Barren acrostics of desolation, chess game
Of twenty-four squares of lust
And twenty-four squares of disgust.
And Jerusalem too like a kettle of roiling stew, a swampy
Porridge, all its buildings—bulging bubbles,
Eyeballs thrusting out of their sockets,
The shape of a dome, of a tower, of a roof, flat or slanted,

All are bubbles before bursting. And God
Takes the closest prophet
As a ladle to stir it, stir it.

I sit here now with my father's eyes
And my mother's graying hair on my head, in a house
That belonged to an Arab who bought it
From an Englishman who took it from a German
Who hewed it from the stones of Jerusalem, my city.
I look at the world of the God of others
Who got Him from others. I am an alloy
Of many things, I was collected in different times,
I was composed of transient parts, of materials
That decompose, words that wear out. And now
In the middle of my life, I'm beginning to return them one by one,
For I want to be a good man, everything in order
At customs, when they ask me: "Anything to declare?"
So there won't be too much pressure at the end,
So I won't arrive sweating, out of breath, confused.
So I won't have anything left to declare.
The red stars are my heart, the Milky Way
In the distance is its blood, my blood. The hot wind
Is blown from big lungs, my life
Is near a big heart, always inside.

I live in the German Colony, called
The Valley of Ghosts, outside they call to each other,
A mother to her children, a child to a child, a man
To God: Come home! Come, come! "And he is merciful"
Come home, God, gather into Your people in Jerusalem
So we can gather into You, in mutual death
And mutual prayers, with waving sheets and smooth pillows,
Turning off the bedside lamp and the eternal light,
Closing the book and closing the eyes, turning
Curled up to the wall. Here in the Valley of Ghosts, in the house
With the year of my birth,
A German phrase carved on its portico: "You start with God
And with God you end. That's all there is to life, my friend."
A stone lion rests and guards the words

And the four-digit number. On the side of the gate
A mezuzah, the flute of my childhood God,
And two pillars, trace of the Temple that was not.
The curtain stirs like the curtain in the hotel in Rome
On that first morning, stirs and is pushed aside,
Revealed to me the groin of that city,
The roofs and sky, and I was seduced to come
To her. Please, now, please. My love, your hair
Is parted in the middle, you walk erect, your strong face
Bears a heavy burden, heavier than the jug
On the head of an Arab woman at the well, and your eyes
Wide open as if burdenless. And outside
Cars wail. Motors adapt for themselves
The voices of people in distress,
In depression, out of gas, in the great heat and in the cold,
In old age and in loneliness, and they wail and weep.

Josephus Flavius the son of dead people, like me,
The son of Matityahu gave up his fortresses in the Galilee
And threw his sword on the table before me:
A ray of light entered from outside. He saw
My name carved on the door as on a tombstone,
He thought my house was a grave. The son of the dead,
Son of the dust, son of the lantern lit in the evening
Outside. The people before my window are Titus's
Legions; they storm Jerusalem on this
Sabbath night, the cafés and the
Cinemas, the lights and the cakes
And the thighs of women: surrender in love,
Supplication of love. The rustle of trees
In the garden announces a change in my feats, but not
In my dreams. My internal clothing will not be changed
And the tattoo from my childhood sinks inside.

*Get thee out*, merry commander and sad historian,
Rest between the pages of your books, sleep in them
Like dry pressed flowers. *Get thee out*, my son too
Is a war orphan of three wars
In which I was not killed

And in which he was not yet born,
Yet he is a war orphan of all of them.
*Get thee out*, white commander of the Galilee. I too
Always come and go as into new apartments,
Through the iron grills of memory.
You have to be a shadow or water
To pass through all that without breaking.
Later, you're gathered again. Making peace
With yourself, a treaty, a contract, everything
As in a real war. Prolonged negotiations
And lengthy sands, trees rustling
Over many war dead, as in a real war.
A woman once told me:
"Everyone goes to his own funeral." I didn't
Understand then. I don't understand now, either, but I'm going.
Death is just a high official ordering
Our lives according to topics and places
In card catalogues and archives. This valley
Is a rift that God tore in mourning
For the dead, and what was left for the poet and the writer
Of history is just to turn over their fortresses
And turn into mourners, for hire or for free.
The fortress of Yodfat opens its gates wide: a great light
Breaks out from there, the light of surrender
That should have been enough for thousands of years of darkness.
Blast, great blow, sad blow,
The lips of the blower cracked in the long hot wind,
His tongue cleaved, his right hand will forget. I
Remember only the motion of the woman
Taking off her dress over her head:
What a raising of arms, what a blind surrender,
What a plea, what passion, what surrender!
"I'm not a traitor," and between the pages disappeared
My brother Josephus. "I have to write history."
The pages are sick, their heads in a leprosy of Hellenistic
Ornaments and in a madness of filigree of flowers and buds.
The home is sick. "Homesick," say the English
When a person is longing for his home. The home
Is mansick. I am longing. I am sick. *Get thee out,*

My brother Josephus, flying flags too
Are curtains in windows that have no home anymore.

I am an Orthodox Jew, my beard grew in,
Instead of flesh and blood, I'm filled with the hair of my beard
Like a mattress. The pain remained unhealed between the phylacteries.
My heart fasts almost every week, whether I dropped a
Torah Scroll or not, whether the Temple
Was destroyed or rebuilt.
I don't drink wine, but all the wine does not
Do inside me is a black hole without drunkenness,
A dark empty wine cellar where the feet trample
The hard stone and are wounded. My body is a dock
For what is called my soul. My body will be dismantled and my soul
Will sail out to sea, its shape the shape of my body
And its shape the shape of the sea,
And the shape of the sea like the shape of my body.

My beloved is a Job. It was in summer, the elastic bands
Of her garments burst like string. The wailing of labor pains
And the gurgle of dying already in the first night of love.
Tearing, a great tearing of light clothing,
For it was summer, the end of a heavy summer of
Light, thin garments. A *shofar* like the retching
Of a sick person. And at the beginning of Elul,
The horn blower blew in a ram's horn and his face was sheepish
Like the ram's face, and his eye bulging and glassy and rolling
In its socket like the eye of a closed tank. And his mouth holds on hope-
	lessly to the *shofar*.
My Job-love, we met in the flight of bitter pollen. In wide spreads
Wider than the spread of wings and beyond the boundaries of your body.
Always in love, despair lies with you now
And your movements and the flutter of your limbs and your screams with
	him
As with me.
Sometimes I feel my soul wallowing
As in an empty barrel. With a muted sound
Of a barrel pushed from place to place. Sometimes
I see Jerusalem between two people

Standing at a window and leaving space
Between them. They're neither close nor in love,
So I can see my life between them.
"If it were possible to catch the moment
When two people begin to be strangers to each other"—

This could have been a hymn
To the sweet, invented God of my childhood.
It was on a Friday, black angels
Filled the Valley of the Cross, their wings
Were black houses and abandoned quarries.
Sabbath candles went up and down like ships
At the entrance to a port. *Come my bride,*
Don the garb of your weeping and your splendor
Of the night when you thought I wouldn't come to you
But I did come. The room reeked with the smell
Of liquor of drunken black cherries.
Newspapers strewn on the floor rustled below
And the pollen of wormwood beat its wings above.
Love with parting, like a record
Of music with applause at the end, love
With a scream, love with a despairing murmur
Of the erect walk into exile from each other.
*Come my bride,* hold in your hand a shard of pottery
At sundown, for flesh melts
And iron wears out. Hold the shard in your hand,
So future archaeologists will find and remember.
They don't know that even anemones after the rain
Are an archaeological find and a major document.

The time has come to close my life as they closed the Bible.
Final decision, chapters, and books remain outside,
Will be apocrypha, days will be counted in the number of days,
There will be ornaments and commentaries and explications
And not the core and not the holy.
I imagine matches wet with tears
Or blood, that will not ignite. I imagine
The blowing of a *shofar* in an assault on an empty target.
A Jewish *shofar* pipe, the Prophet Jeremiah

With a crying head assaulting an empty place.
But on the last Yom Kippur, at the end of the closing prayer,
When all were expecting the *shofar*
In great silence, after shouts of "Open the gate for us,"
A voice was heard like the thin bleating of a baby,
Its first cry. My life, the beginning of my life.

I chose you, I was Ahasuerus sitting
On his throne and choosing. Through the splendid garments
I saw you, the signs of transience in your body
And the portico of the curly hair of the end
Above your groin. You wore black stockings,
But I knew you were the opposite. You wore black dresses
As in mourning, but I saw the red in your body
Like a mouth. I saw the overhanging train
Of red velvet pinched
By the cover of an ancient box that didn't close tight.
I was your bull of Purim and your bullock offering on the Day of
    Atonement,
Wearing shrouds in two colors of a clown.
Broken tones, blast, love, great love.
Sit down. Today the pregnant moment of the world. Who raped
The world so that it is pregnant today.
Today the pregnant moment of the world, today you, today war.

Tanks from America, fighter planes from France, jet doves
From Russia, chariots from England without the riders, Sisyra's legions
That drained the swamps with their bodies, flying Masada,
Betar dropping slowly, Yodfat on wheels, Antonia Capitolina, ground
Ground ground, air ground air, sky
Ground sky. Masada will not fall again, not fall,
Not fall, Masada again, not. Prayer rhymes,
Automatic and single shots. Muezzins armed
With a three-stage missile, tearing of paper and tearing battle cries
Of holy wars of seven kinds,
*Shtreimls* like mines on roads and in the air, philosophical
Depth charges, the heart illuminated with a green light
Inside the motor of a glowing bomber, the chair of the Prophet Elijah
    ejected

In time of danger, throws circumcision knives,
A burning fuse from heart to heart, a Byzantine tank with
A window decorated with an illuminated icon
Pure and soft, mezuzahs filled with explosives,
Don't kiss them lest they blow up, Dervishes
With powdered rococo curls, Job's chief of staff,
His friends, Satan and God in the War Room.
Pricking with flag pins in the living flesh
On hills and valleys made of naked
Humans, lying before them,
Underwater synagogues, periscope rabbis,
Cantors from-the-depths, jeeps armed with women's hair
And the fingernails of wild girls that rip
Lapels in rage and mourning. Supersonic angels
With wings of big fat women's thighs,
Letters of Torah Scrolls in ammunition belts, machine guns,
Flowers in the form of fortified positions,
Fingers of dynamite, false legs of dynamite,
Eight empty casings for a Hanukah lamp,
Explosive memorial candles, a cross of crossfire,
A submachine gun carried on tefillin straps,
Camouflage nets of thin lace of
Panties of beloved women, used women's dresses
And torn diapers for cleaning the muzzle of a cannon,
Attack grenades in the shape of pomegranates,
Defense grenades in the shape of spice boxes
Of Sabbath night, sea mines
Like apples to smell on Yom Kippur
To prevent swooning, half of my childhood
In a whole half-track, grandfather's clock
To activate a time-egg filled
With the cut fingernails of bad children
Smelling of cinnamon, two hands
Clasping each other by Dürer
Like a springing mine, arms with a gadget
For attaching a bayonet, good night fortified
With sandbags, the twelve minor prophets
In a night ambush breathing hot,
Cannon barrels branching like a climbing ivy,

Cuckoo bird shells every quarter of an hour: cuckoo,
Boom-boom. Groins of barbed wire,
Mines of eyes bulging and in pain,
Air bombs with the heads of pretty
Women as on prows of ships in ancient times,
The mouth of a cannon opening like the petals of a flower,
BOOMBOOM, RAMBAM, B52, T72, AK47, STRAIT-TO-HEAVEN,
NATO, SEATO, SALT I, SALT II, PEPPER,
SAM, SCUD, GATT, UNICEF, UNESCO, IONESCO,
UNIFIL, GEFILTE FISH, SATELLITE DISH, TRARARA,
    ETCETERA, ETC.
Sit down. Today the pregnant moment of the world. Today was war.

The horrible angel pulled back his arm
Like a spring to the side of his body, to rest or to swing
A new blow. Keep that arm busy,
Distract its muscles! Hang on it
Heavy jewelry, gold and silver, beads
And diamonds, let it be heavy and drop and not strike
Again. Masada will not fall again, will not fall.

In the fogs that came from below and in the holy bluish
Light, in His great hollow dome,
I saw the Lord of the Earth in all His sadness,
A lonely radar god, turning
His huge wings, with sad movements
Of eternal doubt,
Yes yes, and no no, with the sadness of a god who knows
That there is no answer and no decision except nodding.
Whatever He sees is sad, whatever He writes
Is the script of sadness for people to decipher.
I love the bluish light and the white of His eyes,
White blind screens
For people to read whatever comes into their mind.
Masada again. Masada again. Not again.

On one of these evenings, I tried to recall
The name of one who fell near me in the pale sands
Of Ashdod. A foreigner, perhaps one of the lost

Sailors, who thought the Jewish people is a sea
And these death dunes are waves. The tattoo
Didn't reveal his name, just a flower and a dragon
And fat women. I could have called him
Flower or Fat Women. In the first light
Of retreat and dawn, he died. "In his arms
He died." Thus in Goethe's poem. All evening
At the windows and tables I sank in an effort to recall
As in an effort of prophecy. I knew that if I didn't
Remember his name, I would forget my own, my name would dry up,
"The grass will rise again." That too is from Goethe. The grass
Will not rise again, it will stay crushed,
Stay alive and whispering to itself. Won't rise,
But will never die and will not be afraid of sudden death
Under the soles of heavy jackboots.

In the year when the situation of the world improved
My heart was sick. Will I conclude from this
That my life is falling apart without the hoops
Of danger, sweet and stifling?
I am forty-three. My father is sixty-three.
After the summer comes summer and summer and summer, a
Broken record. To die is when the last
Season will never change.
The body is the wax dripping and gathering and piling up
Of the memorial candle inside me. And Paradise
Is when the dead remember only the beautiful things,
As even right after the war I remembered
Only the beautiful days.

Last spring my child began
To fear for the first time,
Too early, to fear death.
Flowers come out of the ground,
Fear flowers in his heart,
Sweet fragrance to him who enjoys
Smelling this fragrance.
And in the summer I tried to meddle in politics, in the questions of my
    time,

An experience that also has the smell of flowers
And their withering,
A man's attempt to stage and move
Furniture in his home in a new order,
To participate, as in a cinema
When one shifts his head and asks
Those sitting in front of him to shift
Their heads too a bit,
So he has a narrow lane.
At least to see.
I tried to get out to my time and to know, but didn't get
Beyond the body of the woman next to me.
Inevitable. Do not go to the ant, lazy man!
It will depress you to see the blind diligence,
Scurrying under the shoe raised to crush.
Inevitable. As in a modern set of
Chess pieces, made by the artist
With unconventional pieces: the king looks like a queen,
The pawns like knights, and the knights are
Smooth as rooks. But the game keeps
Its rules. Sometimes you long for
The traditional pieces, a king with a crown,
A rook round as a fortress, and a knight, a knight.

The players were sitting inside and the conversation was on the porch:
My half beloved, my left hand, a quarter of a friend,
A man half dead. The sound of the felled pieces
Thrown into a wooden box is like
A distant, ominous thunder.

I am a man getting close to his end.
What seems to be a young spirit in me is not
A young spirit, but a madness,
For only death can put an end to this madness.
And what seems like deep roots I struck
Are only entanglements on
The surface: malady-of-knots and spasm-of-hands,
Confusion of ropes and insanity of chains.

I am a single man, a lonely man. I am not a democracy.
The executive power and the loving and the judicial
In one body. The power that eats and guzzles, and vomits,
The power that hates and the power that hurts
The blind power and the mute power.
I was not elected. I am a demonstration, I raise
My face as a banner. Everything is written out. Everything,
Please, no need to hurl tear gas,
I am already crying. No need to disperse me,
I am dispersed,
And the dead too are a demonstration.
When I visit my father's grave, I see
The tombstones raised by
The dust below:
A great demonstration.

Everyone hears steps at night,
Not just the prisoner, everyone.
Everything at night is steps,
Disappearing in the distance or coming close,
But they never come to you,
Close enough to touch. It is man's mistake
About his god, and God's mistake about man.

Oh, this world, everyone fills it
Up to the end. And the bitter will come and block
Your mouth like a stubborn recalcitrant spring,
So it opens wide, wide, in death.
What are we and what is our life. A child hurt
While playing or hit, holds back his tears
And runs to his mother, in a long way of courtyards
And alleys, and cries only with her.
So all our lives we hold back
Our crying and run a long
Way and the tears are choked in our throat.
And death is merely a good cry
Continuing forever. Blow, great blow,
Great cry, great silence. Sit down. Today.

And the silver hand pointing to the reader
In the Torah Scroll, moves among the difficult lines
Like an arm of a great holy machine.
With its large, twisted, hard finger
It scans and points and hits the words
That cannot be changed. Read here. Die here, here.
And this is the eleventh commandment: Thou shalt not want.

I think about forgetting as about a growing fruit,
If it ripens, it won't be eaten for it won't be and won't be remembered:
Its ripening is its forgetting. When I lie
On my back, the bones of my legs fill up
With the sweetness
Of my little son's breath.
He breathes the same air as I,
Sees the same sights,
But my breath is bitter and his is sweet
As the repose in a weary man's bones,
Blessed be my childhood's memory. His childhood.

I didn't kiss the ground
When they brought me as a little boy to this land,
But now that I have grown upon her,
She kisses me,
She holds me,
She clutches me in love
In grass and thorns, in sand and stone,
In wars and in this spring
Till the final kiss.

# Not
# to Remember

✦✦✦✦ ✦✦✦✦

1971

While the Chosen People
Turns into a nation like all nations
And builds its houses and paves its roads
And opens its soil for pipes and water,
We lie inside the low house,
The youngest children of this old landscape,
The ceiling is vaulted above us in love
And the breath in our mouth is
As it was given to us
And we shall return it.

Sleep is in a place where there are stones.
In Jerusalem there is sleep. The radio
Brings daily sounds from a land where it's day.
Words that are bitter with us
Like an almond forgotten on a tree,
Are sung in a distant land and sweet.

Like fire at night in the hollow olive tree trunk
Not far from the sleeping
An eternal heart burns red.

My love has a long white dress,
Of sleep, of sleeplessness, of wedding,
In the evening, she sits at a small table,
Puts on it her comb, two flagons,
A brush, instead of words.
From the depths of her hair, she extracts many pins
And puts them in her mouth, instead of words.

I mess her hair, she combs it,
I mess it again. What remains?
She falls asleep instead of words,
And her sleep knows me,
Wags its woolly dreams,
Its belly has lightly absorbed
All the raging prophecies
Of the End of Days.

I wake her: we are
The tools of a hard love.

We keep forgetting where we came from. Our Jewish names
From the Diaspora unmask us, evoke memories of
Flowers and fruits, medieval cities, metals,
Knights who turned into stone, many roses,
Perfumes evaporated long ago, precious stones, a lot
Of red, handiwork that vanished from the world.
(The hands too.)

The circumcision hurts.
As in the Torah, in the story of Shechem and Jacob's sons,
We bear the pain all our lives.

What are we doing here, returning with this pain.
The longing dried out with the swamps,
Our desert blooms, and our children are beautiful.
Even shards of ships that sank on the way
Reached this shore.
Even winds did. Not all the sails.

What are we doing
In this dark land casting
Yellow shadows that slice our eyes.
(Sometimes, a person would say after forty
Or fifty years: "The sun is killing me.")
What are we doing with our misty souls, our names,
Our forest eyes, our beautiful children,
Our swift blood?

Spilled blood is not the roots of trees,
But it is the closest thing to roots
Human beings have.

Developing.
Forty-five years developing.

There is already a drink or a dish
Like my name.
When the waiter calls,
I raise my head.

In the narrow alleys there are
Shouts of "out of the way," aimed
Only at me.

Developing,
Constantly unfolding until death.
But my small, old-fashioned soul
Is stubborn:
"I shall not sell a single slice,"
They will never win in a trial against me,
They will have to pave their roads
Around me and on trembling bridges over me.

The tears here do not soften
The eyes. They only hone
And polish the hard face, like a rock.

Jerusalem's suicide attempts.
She tried again on the Ninth of Av,*
She tried with red and fire
And with slow decay of white dust
In the wind. She'll never succeed,
But she'll try again and again.

*The date in the Jewish calendar when both the First and the Second Temples were destroyed.

Our days as in ancient times, in ancient times,
So sighed the light among towers.

Low clouds flying fast,
My friends above.

Vocal cords free from
Throat and rage like an open
Lyre.

Light tickling like eyelashes
On my cheek: (God).

This is the end. What? That's all?
I would like to emit one more laugh,
Once more, to swallow sobs. My sleeve
Has not yet dried at the cuff.

My light gate pretends to be the heavy
Gate of a fortress. I touched it lightly
And it opened. You will speak.

## SUMMER NIGHT IN THE
## KING DAVID HOTEL

Five people were sitting on the balcony.
Their hands rustled like grass.
Five waiters served them:
One, his face like the Old City;
And the second,
In a lighted corner God pays his worshipers
With shining coins.
Five waiters,
One death will serve them,
When the autumn turns into a new year.

But the lovers were lying alongside one another
In the dark. The hand of a blind hot wind
Touched them and shrank back
And confused them and confounded laughter with glass.

Water that never was here suddenly was.
Ancient meditations landed on the wall,
Their banners waving heavily, crockery
Rang, like weapons ready for killing.

Now a slow step walks through the halls,
Its shape like a heart,
Its sound barefoot and damp.

A placenta of love: letters,
Calculations of time, just talk.
I forgot the name of the holiday,
It was warm and good
And I saw you flying without a miracle,
Without an airplane.

Do not ask us
To live a second time.

## POEM ABOUT REPAIRS
### TO MY HOUSE

Taleb, with eyes that saw the gold of Kuwait
And the black cream of oil,
Rehabilitates my house
For a few thousand liras
He exchanges for dinars,
Later, for gold in his eyes.

He raises my fallen roof.
Like an elegant tennis player, he plasters
The walls of my room, changing
The tale of my life.

His feet are on springs. After work
He passes through the Old City.
A sweet river meandering
With a deep, blue coquettishness,
Like ribbons in lush hair. Taleb
Sees an alien woman, her body covered
With gold down: an alien hairy beast, casting
Bouncy shadows in the alleys.
He sees a policeman riding a white horse,
The wings of a parachuted angel on his chest.

Blessed be the summer, burnt grass on the slope:
Conflagration too is a language.

A good time to meet a new
Love is the same time
Good for placing a bomb.

At the juncture
Of season and season,
In blue absent-mindedness,
A slight confusion in the changing of the guards,
At the seam.

Tell them it's not just me,
Others too.
It happened,
And I couldn't change a thing.

Repeat the words again,
Translate them into two or three languages
And look into their eyes, see how understanding
Rises in them. And how it dies like smoke.
And in the end, call in another voice,
A voice that folds into your heart.
Not for them anymore. See
They start their supper. Don't sup with them.
Come back to me.

She grew so big and sad.
Meet her.
Now is a good season
For parting and meeting.

Identify her among the other nights:
What she wears,
What you wear,
What she thinks, what you think.

Sad dancer at two weddings,
Meet her, as at railroad stations,
Recognize her by a whistle, a sign
Agreed in advance,
The color of her dress, her bearing
In the blowing wind, her way of walking,
Of being forgotten among the forgetters.

Not the one of an armistice,
Not even the one of the vision of wolf and lamb,
But,
As in your heart after an excitement:
To talk only of a great weariness.
I know that I know how to kill,
I am grown up.
And my son plays with a toy gun that knows
How to open and close its eyes and say "Mama."
Peace
Without the commotion of turning swords into plowshares, without
   words, without
The sound of heavy seals; let it be light
On top, like lazy white foam.
Rest for the wounds,
Not even healing.
(And the scream of orphans is passed on from one generation
To another, as in a relay race: the baton won't fall.)

Let it be
Like wild flowers,
Suddenly, an imperative of the field:
Wild peace.

Hard men, red-eyed,
Make happy homelands,
Make sad women,
Make playing children,
Far from here in a different sand. At dusk
We stood on the cliff; behind us
The wireless humming. He said:
"I want my son to learn to play the piano.

And over there is Shaduan."
From below came the sound of a soft rumble
Of a cement mixer. From the dugout
At the dismantled fortification. "This concrete block
Begins to feel at home,
Is covered with seaweed like the other rocks."

Here the sky is an archaeological site,
Layers fast moving away, no angels.
And the earth, open pure sky
That holds no memories.

Sated, sated with empty days,
This place with no children,
But I found some of my childhood prayers
Nesting on the shore, like migratory birds,
That remained and didn't return there
(*To the lands of cold, to my window.*)
Reciting the *Shema* in bed, some questions
From the Seder, all those are here, at my feet.

A Jewish ship stands diagonally,
Like a mezuzah, at the entrance to the bay. The bays
Are open to silence, perhaps to peace.

It's too late for all those things.
The eye, in pain, will build
White houses in this place,
Just empty seashells to bring home,
To save ourselves
From the silence.
(Like an empty house talking to an empty house.)

## HYMN TO THE LOVELY COUPLE
### VARDA AND SCHIMMEL

Jerusalem in the week of the marriage of
Schimmel: I saw a beatnik stranger hang his wrapped guitar
On his shoulder, like a rifle.
I saw a beggar hold out his jingling hand
In the door of the public urinal, facing
Men buttoning up. And in the Russian Compound
I heard fresh whores at night,
Singing and dancing in their cells: Estie,
Estie, take me, Estie.

Jerusalem steeped in audiovisual love.
Jerusalem still drunk,
Tourist foam on her lips.

I take her temperature:
38 Celsius in the shade of her armpits.
100 degrees of happiness
In the golden ring.

But matzo!
Schimmel prepares matzo for his wedding.
From the east, 7 red bulldozers cutting
The mountain like a big wedding cake.
10 yellow steamrollers, 30 laborers
With flags and orange fluorescent sweaters.
21 blasts in the afternoon:
Congratulations!

Schimmel and Varda slowly descend
In the parachute of the white synagogue.
Now they stand quietly, wrapped
In the cellophane of God's grace.

Love in one clean room,
Like the dream of years of good life
Compressed into one moment of sleep.
Schimmel and Varda:

Two tranquilizers
Melting slowly in the mouth
Of the excited, collapsing world.

Subtle tools,
Very subtle tools.

And a woman, surprised by light pain,
Something fled from her face inside,
Smile of a shadow.

Her forefathers annihilated Indian tribes:
The guilt of birds
That hurt the air in their flight
Stayed with her.

Subtle tools,
Very subtle tools.

———

Words hanging in a mouth
Like a cigarette unlit,
The migration of birds begins in me,
From my cold heart to my warm heart.
Those do not know
That I am the same man (the birds
Outside know it's the same world.)

"In this room,
Two may be strangers
To one another, as in immense time."

———

Close to Cordoba: I saw
A Jewish girl
From Poland, from Cordoba in Argentina.

In her eyes
I return
To Cordoba in Spain
By a long route.

Echoes of eyelids marked in white
And the chill of musty caves in her eyes
And shadows of long lashes
Like endless fences.

————

Early in the morning, the sun
Is extracted from pillows of dark velvet,
A family treasure, handed down for generations. (Ah!)
An old lamp, a golden samovar,
Refugee of robbery rape
By Cossacks, Indians, missionaries,
Crusaders, Mamelukes.
(Ah!)

Hurry, hurry get up!
Cologne hastily blurred
In the armpit, the neck,
Between the legs still dreaming.
Hurry, hurry, outside! (Ah!)

————

And you live not to remember
But to finish the job
You (in spite of all: you) have to finish.
And not to remain do you love
And not to love are you in pain.

You're fast, weary, impatient
As a day of flying from country to country,
Exchanging good hours of living for ample
Rains, for unknown trade,

Passed on to a lover to a passer-by
On Corientes Street, flowing, flowing.

*Vamos.* In other languages
It is less painful, "let's go"—
There's an illusion of: together,
At first, then: away from each other.

## BALLAD IN THE STREETS
## OF BUENOS AIRES

And a man is waiting in the streets and meets a woman
Precise and beautiful like the clock hanging on her wall,
Sad and white like the wall where the clock is hanging.

And she doesn't show him her teeth
And she doesn't show him her belly
But she shows him her precise and beautiful time

And she lives on the ground floor near the pipes
And the rising water starts in her wall
And he chose softness

And she knows the reasons for crying
And she knows the reasons for restraint
And he begins to look like her, look like her

And his hair will grow long and soft like her hair
And the hard words of his tongue melt in her mouth
And his eyes will shed tears like her tears

And the lights at the crossroads are reflected in her face
And she stands there in the allowed and in the forbidden
And he chose softness

And they walk in the streets that will be in his dreams
And the rain weeps quietly into them as into a meadow
And the crowded time made them into prophets

And he will lose her in a red light
And he will lose her in a green and yellow
And the light is always prepared to serve every loss

And he won't be there when the soap and the cream are finished

And he won't be there when the clock is wound up again
And he won't be when the dress is unraveled into flying threads

And she will lock his wild letters in a quiet drawer
And lie down to sleep near the water in the wall
And she will know the reasons for crying and for restraint
And he chose softness.

# SIGNS AND EVIDENCE IN THE ORCHARD OF GAN-HAYIM

### 1

Face of (a woman),
Face, face of sand between the lines
Of dark trees, like traces
Of a heavy wheel that passed here.
The imprint of a woman's face

And an abandoned shoe full of sky.
Don't worry: it will not
Fill up again with a foot.
It will not go from here.
It is only one shoe.

### 2

Which cloud? The one that was here then. When
Then? Which?
Table, teapot, cloud, all those
In the past tense,
Like passing verbs.
A few swimming motions
Remembered from the last summer.
(To whom to give regards
From whom?)

The clouds put on gold
And were beautiful, or bamboo reeds
Creaking in the dream of a long voyage.
A woman undressing in the rickety hut.
The well-known combination.

The archaeologists went home,
Collected their sticks black and white.
Everything measured.
They left their threads
As secreted webs.

The Roman excavation
Lay gaping on her back,
Abandoned like a woman raped
In the field.
It's all in the open
Though she didn't scream.

If now, in the middle of my life, I think
Of death, I do so out of confidence
That in the middle of death I will suddenly think
Of life, with the same calming nostalgia
And with the distant gaze of people
Who know their prophecies come true.

Half an hour ago
My scream stopped.
Now it's strange and quiet,
Like a factory at night.

I want to make propaganda
For your death.
I sort your letters
Out from the others,
May they live, that are not so long,
Perhaps not so good.
I bring the heavens close
To my eyes, like a myopic man,
To read.

I have a hard time understanding your death in London,
In the fog, just as it is hard for me
To understand my life, here in the bright light.

I smoke a cigarette:
Support for my breathing, so it can be seen from outside.

I read a newspaper silently
And a hand inside me crumbles
A dry, brittle cake,
Heart crumbles heart.

My only chance,
A mistake in the long list,
Forgotten, skipped my name.

## ❧ SOMEPLACE ❧

Someplace
The rain is no more, but never
Did I stand at the border,
Where one leg is still
Dry and the other gets wet in the rain.

Or in a country where people
Bend no more
If something falls to the ground.

218    *Yehuda Amichai*

Great fatigue like that of horses,
If I say horsepower,
It's great fatigue.

My life is a chessboard.
The nights are equal and the white days
Equal and empty.
Pieces were lost or captured.
Rules and laws are no more.
But I feel no joy in the great freedom.

My hand strokes the blank board.
The evening sun covers it with gold
Like the handle of an old box.

### 1

A train pursued by oleanders
Flees between the thighs of hot hills.

Olive trees gape open in panic,
Shake off lizards and chameleons.

The sun gives birth to a sun,
And a sun, and a sun.

Curtain of dust removed, revealing
Stung air kicking in all directions.

Toothless earth, whispering
Crazy thorns, like van Gogh.

### 2

The water mask of the mountains
Burst at night. Hot winds
Come, the true monks,
Essenes from Dead Sea caves,
Come upon us, white, to crack
Lips, dry hearts,
Remind, warn.

### 3

In girls rumpled at noon
You can see the lining of their thoughts.

Behind their eyes,
Hard, white teeth.

With whispering wails
They fall upon me.

With delicate and knowing fingers
They open the orange of my memories
Into pale segments.

With drilling dreams
They reach black oil inside me.

Your eyes withstood great cold
And great heat
Like beautiful glass
And remained clear.

I sat in the happiness. Like straps
Of a heavy knapsack,
Love cut the shoulders of my heart.

Your eyes forced on me
A history of new life.

I sat in the happiness. From now on
I will be just one side in the dictionary,
Expressed or explained.

Your eyes count and count.

Because of hesitations
Between Adar and Nisan, a happy gap
Emerged.

The world is like the moment when
My beloved rummages in her purse,
Searching for the key.
Suddenly a jingle among paper rustling:
Here!

Yes! Toss the words on the table
In a mixed heap
In a Japanese game of thin, colored sticks.
To pull out without moving,
Moved, moved, moved!

On another game: warm,
Warm. Very cold. Less. Now
A bit warmer, warm, cold.

Afterward she licks
Her lips with a sharp tongue,
Passes her finger with a light pressure,
Closes like an envelope.

How many times does a man wait for another man
Who won't come? Three times,
Or four. Then he leaves,
Crosses a field of summer thorns,
And lies in his home.

His heart didn't grow hard, like the soles
Of his feet that walked a lot.
Taxis of dawn tear
The clothes of his sleep:
To live is to tear;
To die, to be torn.

I adorned
Your earlobes, your fingers,
I gilded the time on your wrist,
I hung a lot of bangles on you
To sway in the wind,
To ring quietly above me,
To calm my sleep.

I padded you with apples, as it is written,
So we can roll on a red-appled couch.

I covered your skin with a thin pink cloth,
Sheer as baby lizards
With black diamond eyes in summer nights.

You let me live a few months
Without needing religion
Or a world view.

You gave me a silver letter opener:
This is not the way to open such letters.
You tear them, tear them, tear them.

As in a shoestore
You walk lightly back and forth
On the carpet in front of me.

Does it press? Hurt? Good?
What was there? A café? What scent?

Those, and others, are the questions
To bury whole epochs
In history, the king and his horses,
Burning temples and their priests.

They interpreted your screams
Falsely.

### 1

When Jacob rolled the stone off the well,
Other options were closed,
My history opened.
But my voice remained inside, in the hollow echo.

### 2

Prophet: he himself is rough, he has to
Smooth the world, like sandpaper.

### 3

I think of the miracle
Of splitting the Red Sea, of the children
Of Israel and Pharaoh's army:
The latter drowned in the sea,
And the former in thousands of years of history.
What's better?

### 4

Prophet: God removed the bandage
From his mouth, too soon.

As it was.
When the water we drank at night, afterward
Became all the wine in the world.

And doors I will never remember
Whether they open in or out,
Buttons in the entrance of your house
For light, doorbells, or silence.

We wanted it like that. Did we?
In our three rooms,
At the open window,
You promised me war would not erupt.

I gave you a watch instead of
A wedding ring: round, good time,
The ripest fruit
Of insomnia and eternity.

### 1

Clouds came from the south, the Nile
Overflows its banks. Then there is hope.
War here pretends to be peace,
This shore still believes everything,
Floating papers and all that is written on them,
Seaweed, kelp, gestures of distant,
Foreign nations the waves inherited.
The rock in the water is covered with mold,
Warm as a body under wet wool,
A man carries a tune passing through his shoulder strap.
Long-legged girls like vestiges
Of beautiful houses with tall vaults.
A wind from the sea cools my hot testicles,
I touch the skin of the sand,
I touch the muscles of the sea,
The shadow breaks in a ruin and doesn't tear,
A snake was cut by a glass sliver
And hangs from the wall like the pretty belt
Of a woman undressing.
On a threshold stone, whose house is destroyed,
A watermelon was slaughtered, cracked
And a light face rises
From the heavy tear slowly descending.

### 2

Many dead nations left
Their vestiges here like forgotten clothes at the sea.
This is a convenient place to put my childhood,
To spread the tools of my memories.
In this cracked room, propped up in the middle
By a square pillar, between suspended fishing rods
That dried out long ago, a hurricane lamp forgotten by the hurricane,
Hooks to hold the air, a mast, a net
That hauled in fishermen and fish
Along with my forty-six years.

A man learns to talk in his childhood
So he can talk to himself
When he remains more and more alone,
Talking with others is an ephemeral stage.
Some things grow heavy
Some light, some are anchor and some are sails,
Only after time passes
Do you know which are which.
You don't want any more perspective, you want
Flat calm, not a table
You can put things on, not a house to enter,
But lines, like a child draws, not depth
Promising eternity, not a boulevard with trees
That grow smaller, not a ship vanishing on the horizon.


                                   3

Return begins here. Return
Doesn't have to be to the house
Where you lived, it can be
To a different, distant place.
What do you promise yourself
Standing at the movement of the waves, that reminds you
Of breasts rising breathing excitedly
Of a girl suddenly falling in love, what
Do you promise? Another letter? Calm?
Our names squandered us,
Our roads can go without us.
Perhaps a wandering memory, whose rememberer was lost,
Will find these hours and descend on them,
Your heart counts its moments like a bank teller:
More rustling of paper than ringing of gold,
Than flesh and blood, than the murmur of sea waves.

Strange and superfluous always to take
Everything with you, like a beggar afraid
To deposit his meager belongings in a safe place,
Your hair, your legs, all your memories,
To put your ear to places where there is no sound,
Your liver, your guts,

And everything in them, when you need
Only a mouth, only a caressing hand,
One thought, a single sex organ.
And the more loves you collect,
The more obligations, dependence, arguments,
Claims on your body and soul,
All of you. And it turns out
That what you thought was strong will
Is just the hardness of Jerusalem stones,
When you leave it, you're different.


4

Again and again, you take up your position at the imaginary
Starting line, like chess pieces for a new game,
You're tired. You give yourself
As a secondhand gift, wrapped in pretty paper,
Accepted with no surprise, no cries of joy.

Sailboats and horses remain as toys,
Palmach war songs are played at weddings
Among aunts and insolent beggars.
The sea is calm and big. Your gaze,
Like a beacon directed at the distance,
Strikes the girl sitting near you
And turns her face into illuminated distances,
Without hope of closeness.


5

And thus my belated soul,
Perhaps the last one, begins now to grow on me
From outside, like ivy climbing a house
About to be abandoned, to adorn the ruin.
And there is still hope. Still
The clouds come in the middle of summer
And a young woman brought along her heart
Like a big red ball to play with,
The sea still uses her tanned skin
For its rolling tears, its foamy laugh.

What can you put against all those?
My slow walk, not even love;
My walk is the fifth season that doesn't change.
My face wraps itself in the wind, not to break.
Above me, echoes of supernocturnal voices
And gray hair is gray hair.

# Behind All That Hides a Great Happiness

✹✹✹✹ ✺✺✺✺

1974

*from*

❧ POEMS OF THE LAND OF ❧
ZION AND JERUSALEM

### 2

War broke out in autumn, in the no-man's land
Between grapes and citrus fruit.

Sky, blue like veins in the thighs of a suffering woman.
The desert, a mirror to look at.

Sad males carry traces of their families
In the hump of a rucksack, a sidepack, a soldier's belt,
In sacks of the soul and in heavy bladders of the eyes.

The blood froze in its veins. It cannot spill.
But only break into slivers.

### 4

I have nothing to say about the war.
Nothing to add. I'm ashamed.

The information hurled into me in my lifetime, I
Can relinquish it, as a desert gives up on water.
I forget names I never thought
I would forget.

And because of the war I am saying again
For the sake of the last, simple sweetness:
The sun revolves around the earth, yes,
The earth is flat like a lost board floating up, yes,
There is a God in the sky, yes.

### 6

"Where was he wounded?" You don't know

If they mean a place in his body
Or a place in the land.

A bullet sometimes passes through
A man's body and also wounds
The earth of this land.

7

The blood that stands the member erect
Is not semen.
And spilt blood certainly
Is not seed.

And semen drowning in blood is not seed,
And blood without semen is nothing
And seed without blood is naught.

8

What was the message of the burned man?
Like the message of water:
Not to make noise, or make dirty,
To be very quiet beside it,
To let it flow.

10

Sometimes I think of my fathers
And their fathers' fathers, all that time
From the destruction of the Temple
Through the torments of the Middle Ages
To me. I remember only my grandfather,
He had no extra hands
Or special outlet, or spare navel,
Or instruments to receive and transmit to me.
He was a village Jew, God-fearing,
And hard of seeing, an old man
With a long pipe. My first memory was
When Grandmother, with trembling hands,
Dropped a bowl of hot water on my legs
When I was two years old.

## 11

The city where I was born was destroyed by cannons.
The ship in which I sailed here, was sunk later, in the war.
The barn in Hamadiya where I loved, was consumed by fire.
The kiosk in Eyn-Gedi was blown up by the enemy,
The Ismaeliya bridge I crossed back and forth
On evenings of love, was torn to pieces.
My life is wiped out behind me according to a precise map.
How long can the memories survive?
The girl from my childhood was killed, my father died.

Hence, do not choose me for a lover or a son,
A bridge-crosser, a tenant, a citizen.

## 12

The new homeland was built
On Trumpeldor's last words, "It's good to die for our country,"
Like wild wasps entangled in crazy coils.
Even if those were not his exact words
Or he didn't say them, or they were and evaporated,
Their place remains vaulted like a cave. The mortar
Grew harder than the stones. This is my homeland
Where I can dream without falling,
Misbehave without getting annihilated,
Abandon my wife without being lonely,
Cry unashamedly, betray, lie
Without being hurled to oblivion.

This is the land we covered with fields and forests
And had no time to cover our faces—
They are naked when grief is distorted and joy ugly.

This is the land whose dead are in the soil
Instead of coal, gold, and iron,
And they are the fuel to bring Messiahs.

## 14

I left the Evening Land by the will of the night.
I came late for the cedars, there weren't any more.

I was late for A.D. Gordon and most of the swamps
Were drained before my childhood.

But my restraint from crying reinforced
The foundations. And my legs treading
In the despair of my happiness were like plows
And bulldozers.

And when I grew up, even Our Mother Rachel's voice broke.

My thoughts return to me in the evening
Like the reapers in the days of Degania, covered with dust and happiness,
Atop a wagon.

Now I live in a mountain city where it gets dark
Before it gets dark at the seashore.
And I live in a house where it gets dark earlier than outside.
But in my heart, where I really live,
It's always dark.
Perhaps one day, at the end, there will be light
As in the distant North.

## 15

Even my loves are measured by the wars.
I say, it happened after World War Two,
We met one day before the Six Day War.
I never say, before the peace of '45–'48 or
In the middle of the peace of '56–'67.

But the knowledge of peace
Passes from one place to another
Like children's games,
The same everywhere.

## 32

On the lot that was a short-cut for lovers
A Romanian circus parked.

Near the sunset, clouds huddle
Like refugees in a foreign city of refuge.

A man from the twentieth century
Casts a Byzantine shadow, dark pink.

A woman shades her eyes with a raised hand
Ringing like a raised cluster of grapes.

Pain discovered me in the street,
Whistling to his friends: here's another one.

My father's grave was overrun by new houses
Like tank columns. He remained proud and unvanquished.

A man who has no chance for the Next World
Sleeps with a woman who has.

Their desire, reinforced
By the celibates in the monasteries all around.

This house with love on the frieze
And loneliness for a pillar.

"You can see from the roof" or "Next year"—
Between those two, world and time flow.

In this city, the water level is always
Below the level of the dead.

### 34

Let Memory Mountain remember instead of me,
That's its job. Let the Garden-In-Memory-Of remember,
Let the Street-In-The-Name-Of remember,
Let the famous building remember,
Let the prayer house in God's name remember,
Let the rolling Torah Scroll remember,
Let the memorial remember. Let the flags remember,
History's colorful shrouds: the bodies

They wrapped turned to dust. Let the dust remember.
Let the garbage at the gate remember. Let the placenta remember.
Let the beast of the field and the bird of the sky devour and remember,
Let them all remember. So I can rest.

## 35

In the summer, nations come to one another
To see the nakedness of each other's country.

Hebrew and Arabic,
Like guttural stones and like sand on the palate,
Grew soft like oil for the tourists.

Jihad and a Mitzvah War
Burst like ripe figs.

The network of pipes in Jerusalem protrudes
Like the arteries and veins of a weary old man.

Her houses are like teeth in the lower jaw
Grinding in vain,
For the sky above her is empty.

Maybe Jerusalem is a dead city
Where all the people
Swarm like worms and vermin.
Sometimes they have celebrations.

## 38

*In memory of H.,
who fell in '67
near the bridge of
Gat Shemanim*

And in spite of all that, I must
Love Jerusalem and remember him
Who perished for her on the bridge of Gethsemane,
Whose death was a watershed
Between memory and memory, hope and hope,
Who was the land and the fruit of the land,
A palm branch and trumpets and angels' wings
Were bound up inside him, who was

The salvations and the consolations and the desolations
For the sake of heaven and for the sake of earth,
Who got up and stood, who stood and fell
And his body is another gate in the wall
And his voice a crowd like the crowd at resurrection,
Render unto the sword what is the sword's, unto
Night what is of the night, and unto the din the silence.

Moved by the breath of a sleeping child
He rises now, expanding in a heavenly joy,
And all Jerusalem is a commentary on his death.

As at the beginning of birth:
There's already an opening.
Enough! No more! To rest like this.

People use each other
To heal their pain. Each puts the other
On their existential wounds,
On the eye, the penis, the cunt, the mouth, the open hand.
They grab one another and will not let go.

I have dead people, buried in the air.
I have a bereaved mother while I'm still alive.

I am like a place
At war with time.

Once, the green color rejoiced
Near your face in the window.

Only in my dreams
Do I still love hard.

There is a dark memory, the noise of children playing
Is spread on it like colored sugar.

There are things that will never protect you
Again. And there are doors stronger than graves.

There is a melody, like the one in Ma'adi
Near Cairo, which promised things—
Yet the silence now will try
To keep them in vain.

And there is a place you cannot return to.
A tree blocks the view in the day,
A lamp illuminates it at night,
And more I cannot say
And more I do not know.

To forget and to flower. Flower and forget. That is all.
The rest, sadness of eyes and descriptions of a voyage.

To protect the garden and watch over its fruits
A man must carry his bed on his back like a cross
And put it in the garden and sleep there.
To be part of the shadow in the day and the rustle at night.

And all this is made and built
And planted so you won't fear. Listen,
How the pleas of those
Who want to stay here forever, blend
In the air with the weeping of those who want
To go somewhere else. And all this
Is done properly and it's all good.

And as the earth eroded between
The roots of a tree, I was eroded from my father who stayed.
My sons will again be a rooted tree like him:
Always one generation tree—
And the next, eroded earth.

Heavy with the herd, like our forefathers in the Bible, so
With heavy feelings, smell of sheep and wool,
With heavy hoof steps, in a cloud of dust.
The length of road is divided by time. Nights are divided
Into beautiful bodies: my love and my speed.
And my face breaks, like light, into many colors.
"I remember a deep lovemaking in a week of mourning"
Like desperate knocking on the gate of the dead.

My speech, above, like the rubbing of matches
In vain, in the lost roughness.
And below, between my legs, still noticeable
The clean, elegant scar
Of my circumcision, made by the master
Rabbi Reuven Moshe Eschwege,
Cantor and mohel, the mighty, bald man-bull
Who bent over me gracefully to pluck
My rosy flower with his delicate hands.
A tiny grain in the corner of my eye in the morning
Is all that was left of nights of love,
Of the dust of the roads and the smoke of wars.
Yet I still contribute to the calm
Of my stormy land with the silence of my lips,

And only after my death will you learn
The laws of my life and its motions:
A circle. No, for lines are straight, perhaps
A slight curve. His capacity was such and such. He reached
So many memory years per hour.
He had moments of happiness. He was seasons.

*from*

❧ ELEGIES ON THE WAR DEAD ❧

### 1

Mister Beringer, whose son
Was killed at the Suez Canal, dug
By foreigners for ships to cross the desert,
Is now crossing the Jaffa Gate, near me:

He grew slim: lost
The weight of his son.
He floats lightly in the alley
And grasps my heart like thin branches,
Swept away.

### 4

I found an old book on animals,
Brehm, second volume, Birds:
In sweet language, descriptions of the lives
Of the starling, the thrush, and the swallow.
Many mistakes in old-fashioned Gothic script,
But a lot of love. "Our winged friends,"
"Wandering from us to the warm lands."
Nest, spotted egg, thin down, the nightingale,
The stork, "The heralds of spring,"
The red-breast.

Year of publication, 1913, Germany,
On the eve of war
That was the eve of my wars:

My good friend died in my arms, his blood
In the sands of Ashdod. 1948, June.

Oh, my friend,
Red-breast.

## 5

Dicky was hurt
Like the water tower in Yad Mordekhay.
Hurt. A hole in his belly. Everything
Flowed out of him.

But he remained standing like that
In the landscape of my memory,
Like the water tower in Yad Mordekhay.

He fell not far from there,
A bit to the north, near Huleikat.

## THE NAME OF THE PLACE
### "TRIESTE"

I sat in a café in San Francisco.
The man in a murderer's mask
Is soft inside, like the victim's belly.

The name of the place is "Trieste"
Like the port where my ship sailed
For Eretz Israel.
There I was a young, new nail,
There they hit me as with a hammer
Through the whole Mediterranean
To Eretz Israel.

Nothing disappears in the world:
What was three masts in a ship
Is now three sighs inside me.

# ✦ ASHKELON ✦

A sticky music flows slowly
From the cracks of a café.

Buses groaned in the thicket,
Between their fat tires, like women with wide-spread legs.

The eye of God watches from above like a scoop of ice cream
That will not melt or diminish.

Children go in and out of the womb,
Their skin shining.

Knees too are the horns of an altar
To bind the holiday with strong and loving despair.

My first wife is there too,
But her face is covered with a veil of distance.

And my life is a long night
Where the days pass like fish in the light.

The white sand
Is ideal material for God.

But the soul no longer lives inside.

A government that died long ago once decided
To plant oleanders near the train stations.
Some of them already closed, the tracks dismantled,
But the oleander stayed and grew. The flowers
Of the rash decision of a former official, a beautiful
Commentary on iron, smoke, and parting. There is hope,

Perhaps in the Byzantine period
With the fish and the glass,
And lying inside the eyes
Of hot tears of happiness.

Or in Ramatayim where I saw
Two old people describing to one another
The migrations of pain in their body,
And two young people their love:
It's here in the chest. Like pressure. It's
Warm in the throat. "Where is it in you?"
In the belly. Here. Soft. Touch it. Touch it.

Softness of spring in the yard.
A blossoming tree, four girls playing
Between two lessons of the Holy-Tongue
Before a memorial wall of marble:
Levi, Sonnino, Cassuto, and the others,
In straight lines as in a newspaper
Or a Torah Scroll.

And the tree stands in memory of nothing,
Just in memory of this spring,
Arrivederci, *avinu,**
Buona notte, *malkenu.*

Tears in the eyes
Like dry crumbs in the pocket,
Of a cake that was.

Buona notte, Sonnino,
Arrivederci, the six million,
The girls, the tree, the crumbs.

*avinu*—"Our Father"; *malkenu*—"Our King" (beginning of a prayer).

## A CZECH REFUGEE
## IN LONDON

In a very short, black velvet skirt,
A refugee from police regimes (her father still imprisoned there).
Her cunt is very strong, like the only eye
Of a war hero.
She strides, a strong woman with white thighs,
Under this gray sky. "Everyone in his time
Does his deed." In our country, a lot of deserts
With caves and nooks to hide in.
"Does his duty."

She behaves here like a textbook for a foreign language:
She gets up in the morning. Washes. (She
Does not think about me.) She dresses.
She returns in the evening. She reads.
(She will never think about me.) She sleeps,

"When the air softens in late spring,
Every year I discover: I have no defense."

Dennis was very sick.
His face withdrew,
But his eyes advanced from their sockets
With excited courage.
As in war,
When fresh reinforcements
Pass by defeated troops
On the way to attack.

He must get well fast.
He's like our bank
Where we deposited what we had in our hearts.
He's like Switzerland,
Full of banks.

He can already smoke one cigarette,
Trembling a little,
And as befits a true poet
He returns the burned matches
To the box.

**1**

Voices dispersed in the gardens long ago.
Those who have a home returned home.

In waiting rooms suffused with white light
Prophets wait for the dark of the End of Days.

Figs melted the paper bag,
Grapes break out of a thick prison.

A priest explains the crucifixion in a whisper at dusk.
Thunder of roses rolls from black gardens in the sky.

An empty love will fill up with the rains of coming winter.
Through a thick oleander bush, a man enters his home.

A fat woman who lost her husband in the war
Talks with the sweet, thin voice of a child.

A lonely man picks up a button in a backyard,
Looks at it, and it's red.

A great forgiving suckles with love
An infant pink sin.

A chronic adulterer leans his forehead
On a wall and weeps.

**2**

In an unfinished house
Stands a finished woman.

She parachuted here through her hair.
She is seen in a frameless window.

She knows the place of ground water.
In our grief, she is silent with open lips.

She creates quiet facts like history,
Turning what's happening into quiet past.

She lulls her hurting steps to sleep.
A purple tree blossoms for her somewhere else.

There, big nails are lying, whitewash and plaster,
Like God who abandoned the earth and left traces.

An old man paints veins of marble
On a smooth, naked wall.

### 3

A girl smells of a burned field:
Her lips are beautiful like an ancient, forgotten tongue.

Frankincense builds a high nest. In her hair
A breeze blows light kisses on her skin.

Narrow alleys squeeze her till sweet sweat.
An old Ottoman law melts in her eyes.

With a light, sandaled step, she forgets heavy days.
In her armpit she crushes a white pillow for sleep.

Her evening face changes into her night face.
A stranger watches the changing of the guard.

A roof crushed by people celebrating in midnight.
The voice of the drum and the flute is heard.

The dancers in the house are stars
In an open box of a star collector.

Guests fly out the gate,
Their faces changed to tranquillity, like the dead.

A heavy silence leaps into an empty bed,
A stranger sits in a chair all night and sighs.

4

A dead man rides his bicycle,
Won't sway, straight and calm.

Longing placed in the window
Like flowers in the day, like a lamp in the night.

Words anoint each other with oil
In the misty rooms of the sun.

A man remembers with closed eyes
What happened to him a little while ago.

A woman combs the hair of another woman
And she too weeps before the mirror.

6

A shepherd strolls in the woods, beautiful
Like the young bachelors and virgins in the mountains of Benjamin.

His fins shine in the evening
He walks by without a face.

His goats were shed between the carob trees
A sheep of grapes stands holy in the moonlight.

A peasant sows into the past century
Swinging backward, as in pictures of the pioneers.

An old Arab takes a grandchild, an oud, and a donkey,
Wanders in villages that once were,

Sings of a camel with high eyes
Who went to seek the love of his soul.

In the orchards, the tick-tock of the pump stopped.
A blue light lies in the night and feels cold.

# *Time*

❋❋❋❋ ❋❋❋❋

1978

Poems of continuity, mines and graves,
Revealed when they build a house or a road:
The raven people from Meah Shearim come black
To squawk bitterly: "Corpse, corpse." Then young soldiers
Arrive, with hands from last night,
Dismantle the iron and decipher the death.

So let us not build a house or pave a road!
Let us make a house folded in our heart and a road
Scrolled on a reel in our soul, inside,
And we shall never die.

People live here inside fulfilled prophecies,
As in a heavy cloud after a blast that didn't disperse.
In their lonely blindness, they touch each other
Between legs, between day and night,
For they have no other time and no other
Place, and the prophets died off long ago.

On this evening, I think again
About many days sacrificed
For one night of love.
About the waste and the fruit of waste,
About plenty and about fire.
And how without pain, Time.

I saw roads leading
From another man to another woman.
I saw life erased
Like a letter in the rain.
I saw a table with leftovers
And wine with the label "brothers"
And how without pain, Time.

※ 4 ※

My son was born in Asuta hospital and since then
I follow him in his life, as much as I can.

Son, when the schools leave you alone
And you remain bare, when you see life
Fall apart at the seams, and the world
Unhinged, come to me,
I'm still a great expert in confusion and tranquillity.

Like a calm album, its pictures
Torn out or fallen out, yet its weight is the same,
I am still the same man, almost with no memories.

The aching bones of lovers
Who rolled all day in the grass.

Their lying together, awake at night,
Brings redemption closer to the world. Not to them.

A bonfire, blind with pain, repeats in the field
The sun's act in the day.

Childhood is far away.
War is close. Amen.

The soldiers in the grave say: you, up there,
Placing a wreath upon us,
Like a lifesaver of flowers,
See how our faces all look alike
Between stretched out arms. But
Remember the differences that were between us
And the joy on the water.

What is it? An old shed for tools.
No, it's a great love that was.
Fear and happiness were in this darkness,
And hope. Perhaps I was here once,
I didn't get close to see.

Those are calls from a dream.
No, it's a great love.
No, it's a shed for tools.

*How goodly are your tents, Jacob.* Even when there are no
Tents and no Jacob, I say: How goodly.

Oh, let something redeeming come, an old song,
A white letter, a face in a crowd, a door
Open to the eye, ice cream colorful to the palate,
Oil for the intestines, a remembrance warm to your heart.

Then my mouth is open always to praise
Like the gaping belly of a calf hanging on a hook
In a butcher shop, in the *souk*, in the Old City.

Advice of good love: do not love
Women far away. Take one nearby,
As the right house takes stones
From its own place, stones that suffered in the cold
And glowed in the sun and were scorched.
Take the one with the golden wreath
Around her dark pupil, who knows something
About your death. You must love even
Among the ruins, like the honey
In Samson's devastated lion.

And advice of bad love: with the redundant
Love, left from the last one,
Make yourself a new wife, and with
What's left of her, make yourself
A new love,
Till nothing's left.

Shifra and Batya promised
With their loins eternal youth.

The years of their birth are so fresh.
They fill their thighs with a sweet tension
And my brain with a sound, like a bright chord.

They said: men are strange and crazy:
A sword that comes to kill, they adorn
With ornaments and diamonds

And the penis that brings joy
They don't.

How did a banner begin? Let's assume there was something whole
Like the dress of a woman you yearn for. Then it tore
In two, and was enough for two warring camps.

Or like a lounge chair in an abandoned garden
From my childhood, torn stripes waving in the wind,
This too is a banner, telling you to get up and follow it
Or cry near it, betray or forget.

I don't know: in my wars, the standard-bearer did not go
Before the gray host in clouds of dust and smoke.
I saw things that began like spring
And ended in hasty retreat in pale sand.
Now I am far from it all, like a man
In the middle of a bridge who forgets both its ends
And remains leaning on the parapet
Watching the waters flowing below,
They're a banner too.

The radius of the bomb was twelve inches
And the radius of its effective force seven yards
Containing four dead and eleven wounded.
And around those, in a wider circle
Of pain and time, are scattered two hospitals
And one graveyard. But the young woman,
Buried in the place she came from,
Over a hundred kilometers from here,
Widens the circle quite a bit,
And the lonely man mourning her death
In the provinces of a Mediterranean land,
Includes the whole world in the circle.
And I shall omit the scream of orphans
That reaches God's throne
And way beyond, and widens the circle
To no end and no God.

I am the figure of a Jewish father with a sack on his back, returning
Home from market. I have a rifle hidden
Among soft things in a cabinet with the perfume of a woman's lingerie.
I am a man afflicted with the past and sick with the future. An inflamma-
tion of the present
In his red eyes, a futile guard against evil,
A useless guard against death, watching sweet Jewish meat
Like the meat of any persecuted game. And in the evening, he hears
Church bells rejoicing at Jewish woe,
And from the hills a sad brigade exercise,
Their cannons have roots instead of wheels.
And he buys cream for his shoes and his parched
Lips, and he smears it for the sake of tranquillity.

And in his coat, documents of mercy and papers of love,
And he sees people on their hasty road from the past to the future,
And at night, alone and slowly, he cooks jam
Stirring, all around, till it thickens
With big bubbles like Jewish eyes
And white sweet foam for future generations.

What is it? An airplane at dawn. No,
They're digging a sewer in the sky. No, it's
A deep rift along the wonderful nightingale. No,
It's the raucous screwing of a he-bulldozer and a she-bulldozer.
No, it's a peacock shrieking: this beautiful bird
Shrieks so bitterly. But it's a quiet hymn.
No, it's the consolation of mourners humming like a teapot
On a low flame. And now an explosion!
No, it was a nightingale, heavy and hollow.
It seems like night. No,
It's a lark heralding the rising sun.
It's the dawn of nations.
No, it's my friend the quiet artillery man whistling
And feeding home cannons with shells at dawn.

What is it? It's the misunderstanding of love:
Don't be scared, child, the dog loves you,
He just wants to play with you. Just
A misunderstanding of love, like our tears
At the ancient window overlooking the valley.

From the Scroll of Esther, I filtered out the sediment
Of coarse joy, and from the book of Jeremiah
The wailing of pain in your guts. And from
The Song of Songs, the endless search
Of love, and from Genesis
The dreams and Cain, and from Ecclesiastes
The despair, and from the Book of Job, Job.
And from the leftovers, I pasted together a new Bible for myself.
I live censored, pasted, limited, in peace.

One woman asked me yesterday in a dark
Street about the health of another woman
Who died before her time, or anybody's time.
In great weariness I answered:
She's fine, she's fine.

My friend, what you're doing now
I did a few years ago.
The time that has since passed equals the difference in our ages.

You see me stiff-eyed and soft-necked
And my sex organ is the last bridgehead
To a new generation of young women.

Afterward, clearing the remnants of love
And trash of happiness, like any disturbing garbage.

I see you desperately clutching everything around you,
Books, children, wife, musical instruments,
And you don't know that all this is just gathering branches
To your body for the great bonfire where you will burn.

I was weaned from the curse of Adam.
The flaming sword is far away
And flickers in the sun like a propeller.
I already love the taste of salty sweat
On my bread with dust and with death.

But the soul that was given me, is still like a tongue
Remembering sweet tastes between the teeth.

And I am already the second Adam, banished
From the Garden of the Great Curse where
I made do after the Garden of Eden.

And under my feet, a small cave grew
In the precise shape of my body.
I am a man of refuge: the third Adam.

## ❊ 32 ❊

When I was young, the country was young too. My father
Was everybody's father. When I was happy, the country was happy, when I
    jumped
Upon her, she jumped under me. The grass that covered her in spring
Softened me too. Her soil in summer pained me
As parched skin in my soles. When I loved
Immensely, her independence was announced, when my hair
Waved, her banners waved. When I fought,
She fought. When I rose, she rose too, and when I declined
She began declining with me.

Now I part from all that.
Like a thing glued on to something when the glue dries up,
I separate and roll into myself.

Recently I saw a clarinet player
In the Police Orchestra playing in David's Tower.
His hair white and his face calm: a face
From 1946, that sole year
Between famous and terrible years
When nothing happened but a great hope and his playing,
And me lying with a girl in a quiet room in Jerusalem nights.
I haven't seen him since then, but the hope
For a better world hasn't left his face, till now.

Later, I bought some nonkosher sausage
And two rolls and went home.
I heard the evening news,
Ate and went to bed,
And the memory of first love came to me
Like a feeling of falling before you fall asleep.

Oh, my old, venerable teacher, life
Is not deep, as you said. History
And the love of Buber and Marx are just
A thin crust of paved road on the great earth.

Oh, my teacher, the boundary of toys is so close:
When a rifle shoots and kills, and father really died.

And the boundary of camouflage, which is also the boundary
Of love: instead of a cannon, a real tree
Grows. And she will be I, and I—she.

The door of the house opened by mistake:
"You shouldn't have been here now."

A thin whistle in the dark:
It was a young fig tree.

A slight despair raised its head, for a moment,
Like a watchdog, though it didn't bark.

Rapists slept in the forest
And dreamed of true love.

You shouldn't have been here.
But now I am here.

We floated together to the springs of your madness,
A turbulent waterfall. In the morning, calm water.

In the garden, at the white table
Two corpses sat in the heat of the day.
A branch moved above them. One pointed
To things that never were.
The other spoke of a great love
That has a launching pad even after death.

If we can say so, they were
A pleasant, cooling sight
On that hot day, with no sweat
And no voice. Only when they got up to go
Did I hear them as the clink of china
Cleared from the table.

I am like a leaf that knows its limits
And doesn't want to extend beyond them,
Not to blend with nature, not to flow into the big world.

I am so quiet now that
I can't imagine
I ever shouted, even as a baby in pain.

And my face, what is left
After they hewed it for love,
Like a quarry. Now abandoned.

Karl Marx, cold mark that you are,
A man outside and a Jew in your grave in the alien rain.
"Man will live by bread alone": you yourself, bread alone,
Lonely bread that you are,
A round loaf from the last century,
A rolling loaf turning everything upside down.

I'm here, on this winter day in Jerusalem,
Where weary Jews seek on their body,
Shoulder bones, chest, belly, and genitals: danger and love.
My skin still protects me from the rain,
But if I still cry, one of my tears will hold
This water coming down now from the skies.

Karl Marx with a beard, like a Hasidic rebbe, slaughterer
And examiner of history, so it will be kosher, according to the law.
Look, I put a lamp near my window to make myself
An area of light, I pay rent on time,
This too a line of defense, right beyond it enemy armies
With missiles and thunder, the final battle
And the first death with nothing after it.
Look, my love caresses my breast,
The hairy side of my feelings.

Karl Marx, the final drop
Is always a tear.

＊ 41 ＊

The evening is lying at the horizon, donating blood.
Flocks of birds flutter up, like black mist.

Love is a reservoir of grace and pampering,
Like the granaries and pools in a siege.

A child sits alone in his bed,
His kingdom the kingdom of all worlds.

People build a fence around their house,
So their hope won't be in vain.

In a white, closed room, a woman
Decides to let her hair grow again.

The earth is turned up for seed.
A secret military installation blooms in the dark.

These words, like heaps of feathers
At the edge of Jerusalem, on the rim of the Valley of the Cross.
In my childhood, there sat the women pluckers,
Thus these words fly into the world.
The rest is slaughtered, eaten, digested, rotten and forgotten.

Androgynous time, neither day nor night,
Erased this valley in his green gardens,
And once there were love experts
Who made it there in the dry grass on summer nights.

That's how it started. Since then, a lot of words
And a lot of loves. Buying a lot of flowers
For warm hands and to adorn graves.
That's how it started, and I don't know how it will end.
But still beyond the valley, from pain and distance,
We shall call to each other forever: "We shall change!"

## ➤ 43 ◈

A hymn for Independence Day. So distant,
Yet everything still remembered, like the echo of steps
Whose bodies long ago turned into dust in the Negev.
The trumpets I hear now, are not for me anymore.
Even their warm breath is not for me.
And the remembered dust turned into forgetting fields.

Builders and destroyers meet at my home in the evening
To sit all night on the porch
Watching the fireworks that are
The colorful sighs of the Jewish people.

Let us not talk about the famous six million,
Let us talk about the eleven who remained,
Let us talk about one of them,
Myself:
I am a man-hill.
Yet in all my strata
Something
Still moves.

You carry the load of heavy buttocks and your eyes are light.
On your loins, a wide belt that will not protect you.

You are made of materials that slow down
The joy and its pain.

And I already taught my sexual organ
To speak your name, like a clever bird.

You're not amazed, as if you didn't hear.
What else was I supposed to do for you?

Now, only your name stays with me,
On its own, like a beast:

Eats from my hand and sleeps at night
Curled up in my dark brain.

Jerusalem the cradle city that rocks me.
When I wake up things happen to me in the middle of the day
As to a man descending the stairs of his lover's house
For the last time and his eyes are still shut.
But my days force me to open my eyes and to remember
The faces of passers-by: maybe he will love me,
Maybe he planted a bomb wrapped like a package
Gift-wrapped for a lover. I see
The flaws in the stone buildings, the hole
Through which electricity flows, the slit for water,
The nakedness of the telephone connection and the sighing mouths.

I am a man of Jerusalem. Swimming pools and their voices
Are not part of my spiritual life. Dust is my consciousness,
Stone my subconscious,
And all my memories are closed yards on summer afternoons.

Evening hours of the soul
Fell upon me in the morning.

Soft walking on lush grass like hope
For something. The shoe always remains hard.

A child stands unmoving in the field
And I don't know that he's more eternal.

A man with two futures weeps with sudden fear,
A man empty of memories fills up his body, not to be swept away.

A woman reads a letter at a window
And changes beyond recognition.

A door opens and closes and opens.
Another door remains shut: through it, the silence.

A trap rises from the earth on a summer night,
A soaring trap stretching its wings.

A computer rolls its eyes upward,
Like tormented and blissful saints.

Hoarse girls attracted men
With their hoarse voices to their outings.

In the lighted house, lovers tear
Each other into tatters of flesh, dripping quiet blood.

In the garages of the Kidron Valley
A black hearse is repaired.

An orphaned father puts his little boy on his lap
And sings him a lullaby for his sins.

The eyes of the sleeping people are mines:
The first morning light will set them off.

The man crossing the field was a Chief Rabbi
In Africa. And I once was the chief lover
In my home. In spite of his years, he makes himself
A new future here, with rigorous strolls
In the Judean Mountains. He learns. He
Sees one wisdom of life that heaps
Stones into a fence and another wisdom
That scatters them again over the hill.
He sees a burned field and learns
That a burned field will not burn again.
This too is hope and great repose.

These things are well known,
Like the blowing wind or
Like Rachel mourning her sons in her grave.

Early in the morning, you lean on the wall of an old house,
A strong buttress. Later you will lightly jump
Into a bus with the other jumpers.

In such holy shoes, you
Go to work in an office every day,
In such love clothes, to be widened and narrowed.

What protects you? Very thin stockings
Up to your belly button.

What holds up the old house?
A memory. Until you come again
To lean on it the next morning.

When a man is away from his homeland for a long time
His language becomes more precise, correct, with no mistakes,
Like well-defined clouds in summer
On a blue background that will never rain.

So those who were once lovers sometimes
Still speak a love language, barren and pure
Of everything, neither changing nor yielding.

But I, who remained, use a dirty
Mouth and lips and tongue. In my words there is
Soul dung and passion garbage and dust
And sweat. Even the water I drink
Between my screams and the murmur of passion,
In this dry land, is the water I make,
Recycled to me in a convoluted way.

I love these people in their tall house
In the north. From their window you can see
The ships in their proud voyage
To an even farther north,
And what cannot be seen in the window doesn't exist.

Many islands and not a single memory.
The forests always in rain.
The only evidence, the lush fern,
An ancient reminder, preferably forgotten.
And in the clearing of the woods, wet leaves and mire,
A warm and misty lover's nest.

"I am the soul of the landscape," said
One woman. And the other one too,
And another one, and another one.

Late in my life, I come to you,
Filtered through many doors, diminished
By stairs. Almost nothing is left of me.

And you are such a surprised woman,
A beast with half a courage.
An untamed woman with glasses,
The elegant harness of your eyes.

"Things tend to get lost and be found again
By others. Only people love
To find themselves," you said.

Later, you broke your whole face
Into two profiles, one for the distances,
And one, a souvenir for me. And you went.

You're small and thin in the rain. A small target
For the drops and for the dust in summer
And for shrapnel. Your belly is soft,
Not the skin of a drum, flat and taut: the softness
Of the third generation. Your grandfather, the pioneer, drained swamps.
The vengeance of the swamp is upon you. You're full of
Craziness, drowning and bubbling in rainbow colors.

And what will you do now? You'll collect loves
Like stamps. You've got doubles and no one
Will trade with you and you have damaged ones.
The curse of your mother hovers over you, like a strange bird.
You look like her.

Your room is empty. Every night your bed
Is made. It's the bed's punishment of hell:
To be without a sleeper in it,
No crease, no stain, like the cursed summer sky.

My son, the softness of your face already shows
The first eagle's courage, the advance of your cheeks,
Let me kiss you one more time, when you still
Love it, softly like this.
Before you become a hairy Esau of the fields,
Be a little more Jacob to my blind hand.

Your brain is well packed in your head,
Efficiently folded for life. Had it remained
Stretched, maybe you'd be happier,
A huge canvas of happiness without memory.

I am on my way from belief and you
On your way to it. This too
Is an encounter between father and son.

It's evening now, the globe cools off.
Clouds that never slept with a woman
Pass above us in the sky. The desert
Begins breathing near our ears
And all the generations extort a holiday
Of bar mitzvah for you.

In this valley, where many waters
Over endless years dug into it
So a light breeze would go through it now
To cool my forehead, I think about you.
From the slope, I hear voices
Of man and machine, wrecking and building.

There are loves you cannot
Transfer to some other place.
They have to die in their own place and time,
Like an old, clumsy piece of furniture
That will be destroyed with the house it stood in.

But this valley is a chance
To start again without dying. To love
Without forgetting the other love
And to be like the breeze passing it now
Though it was not meant for it.

"He left two sons," they say
Of a man who died. Sometimes still alive.

The echo of a great love that was, like the echo
Of a big dog barking in an empty house
Slated for demolition in Jerusalem.

My former student is in the traffic police.
She stands at a crossroads in the middle of the city:
She opens a little cupboard, like a makeup cabinet
And changes the colors of the traffic light according to her mood.
Her pupils, an assortment of green, red, and yellow,
And her hair is very short, like an insolent boy's.
With her black, high shoes, she leans
On the cabinet. Her skirt is short and tight
And I don't even dare imagine
The awesome splendor at the end of all that golden brown.

I don't understand anymore. I'm lost.
When I pass in the street, legions of young men
And women are hurled at me, every year
In increasing waves, endless reserves.
And my student the policewoman couldn't stop them.
She even joins them!

What a man on a bald mountain in Jerusalem!
A scream opens his mouth, a wind rips
The skin of his cheeks and pulls it back,
Like a harness in an animal's mouth.

His message of love:
Increase and multiply, a sticky business,
Like candy on a child's fingers, attracts flies,
Or like a tube of dried-out shaving cream,
Cracked and half empty.
His threats of love:
On your back! You! With all
Your extremities and trembling antennae! Just wait, I'll push
Inside you up to your grand-grandchildren!
And she'll answer him:
Those will bite you there
Inside me. They will be stiff rodents,
My last descendants.

"But a man is not a horse," my cobbler said to me.
He repaired my stiff new shoes
And softened them. And suddenly
I cried
From so much love poured all over me.

And I am always like this fleeing from hurt and pain,
From the sweating touch and the hard affront.
Most of my years in Jerusalem, a bad place to avoid
All that. And all my wars in deserts
Among hard stones and wounding gravel.
I never got a war in a cool, green forest
Or a wavy sea battle.

Thus, fleeing, evading, like a wretched dancer
Between the stoning and the shells,
Between the strong hand and the outstretched arm,
A clumsy man in his flight, with a heavy load.
My whole body is taken from head to toe:
On my back a rifle, a sack camouflages my forehead,
On my belly an ammunition belt. On my head
Guilt, and my feet in cages of shoes,
On my shoulders the yoke of family and even my knee
Sets off the motor of a terrible time as I walk.
Only my sex organ is still free and happy,
No good for the swords of war and not fit
For any profession, and you can't hang
Straps on it or reinforce a fortress.
Thank God for that. (I burdened even God with thanks.)

And so, too heavy, I flee
To the last pain that won't hurt anymore.

My God, the soul you gave me
Is smoke
From the eternal fire of love memories.
We are born and start burning right away,
Until the smoke vanishes like smoke.

Then I went down to the ancient port: human actions
Bring the sea closer to the shore, other actions
Move it away. How should the sea know
What they want. Which jetty holds it like love
And which one pushes it away.

In the shallow water, lies a Roman pillar.
This is not its final place. Even if
They take it from here and put it in a museum
With a little explanatory label: it'll go on falling
Through floors and strata and other times.

But now, a wind breezing through the tamarisk trees
Blew the final red heat in the faces of those sitting here
As in the embers of a dying bonfire. Then, night and whiteness.
The salt eats into everything and I eat
Salt, until it does me too.
Then, what was given to me is taken back and again
Given, and what was thirsty was satisfied,
And what was satisfied, long ago rested in death.

# Great Calm:
# Questions and Answers

✦✦✦✦ ✦✦✦✦

1980

Forgetting someone is like
Forgetting to turn off the light in the yard,
It stays on all day:
And that means also remembering—
By the light.

## ❧ SINCE THEN ❧

I fell in the battle of Ashdod
In the War of Independence.
My mother said then, He's twenty-four years old,
And now she says, He's fifty-four,
And lights a memorial candle
Like birthday candles
On a cake, to blow out.

Since then, my father died of pain and sorrow,
And my sisters got married
And named their kids after me,
And since then my home is my grave, and my grave—my home.
For I fell in the pale sands
Of Ashdod.

And since then all the cypresses and all the orchard trees
Between Negba and Yad Mordekhay
Walk in a slow funeral procession,
And since then all my children and all my forefathers
Are orphans and bereaved parents,
And since then all my children and all my forefathers
Walk together arm in arm
In a demonstration against death.
For I fell in the war
In the soft sands of Ashdod.

I carried my comrade on my back.
And since then I feel his dead body always
Like a sky weighing heavy upon me,
And he feels my bent back beneath
Like a convex segment of the globe.
For in the terrible sands of Ashdod, I fell
Not just he.

And since then I compensate myself for my death
With love and dark feasts,
And since then I am of-blessed-memory,
And I don't want God to revenge my blood.
And I do not want my mother to cry over me
With her beautiful, precise face.
And since then I fight the pain,
And I walk against my memories
As a man walks against the wind,
And since then I mourn my memories
As a man mourns his own death,
And since then I extinguish my memories,
As a man puts out a fire,
And I'm quiet.
For I fell in Ashdod
In the War of Independence.

"The feelings raged!" they used to say then, "The hopes
Ebbed," they used to say, but no more,
"The arts flourished," said the history books,
"Science prospered," they said,
"The evening wind chilled their hot foreheads,"
They said then,
"The morning wind swayed their forelocks,"
So they said.
And since then the winds do different things
And the words say different things
(Do not see me as if I were alive),
For I fell in the soft, pale sands
Of Ashdod in the War of Independence.

## AN ARAB SHEPHERD SEEKS
## A KID ON MOUNT ZION

An Arab shepherd seeks a kid goat on Mount Zion,
And on the mountain across, I seek my little son.
An Arab shepherd and a Jewish father
In their temporary failure.
Our voices meet above
The Sultan's Pool in the valley between us.
We both want to prevent
Our son and our kid from falling into the process
Of the terrible machine of Had Gadya.

Later, we found them in the bushes,
And our voices returned to us
And cried and laughed inside us.

The search for a kid or a son
Was always
The beginning of a new religion in these mountains.

## ON THE WIDE STAIRS— LURKING FOR HAPPINESS

On the wide stairs going down to the Western Wall
A beautiful woman came toward me: "You don't remember me,
I am Shoshana in Hebrew. Different in other languages.
It's all vanity." So she said in the twilight and stood
Between the demolition and the construction, between light and dark.
Black birds and white birds traded places
In a quick-breathing tempo.
The flashes of tourist cameras jogged my memory too:
What are you doing here between the promised and the forgotten,
Between the hoped-for and the imagined?
What are you doing here lying in wait for happiness
With your beautiful face from God's tourist advertising
While your soul is as tormented and torn as mine?

She answered: My soul is as tormented and torn as yours
Yet it became more beautiful,
Like fine lace.

Holiday mourners, we are name-engravers on stones,
Hope-infected, hostages to governments and history,
Blown with the wind and vacuum inhalers of holy dust,
Our king is a beautiful weeping child,
His picture hangs everywhere.
Stairs always make us
Jump as in a merry dance, even
Those who are sad and heavy-hearted.

But the heavenly couple sits on the porch
Of the café: his arm strong and ready,
She with long hair. They are relaxed now,
After the offering of halvah and honey and hashish incense
Both wear long, transparent gowns
Without a thing underneath.
When they rise up from their rest, facing the sun
Setting in Jaffa Gate, everybody stands
And looks at them:
Two white halos around dark bodies.

The eternal mystery of oars
Plowing back as the boat floats forward,
So our deeds and words plow toward the past
For the body to go forward with the person inside.

I once sat in a barber's chair at the edge of the street
And in the big mirror I saw people come toward me
And suddenly disappear, swallowed by an abyss
Beyond the big mirror.

And the eternal mystery of sunset in the sea:
Even a professor of physics, who knows, says:
Look, the sun sets in the sea, red and beautiful.

Or the mystery of words like
"I could have been your father" or
"What did I do a year ago today?"
And other words like these.

Joys have no parents. Not a single joy
Learned from an earlier one, and each dies without heirs.
But sadness has an old tradition,
Passing from eye to eye, heart to heart.

And what did I learn from my father: to cry fully, to laugh out loud,
And to pray three times a day.
And what did I learn from my mother: to close my lips, my collar,
Cupboard, dream, suitcase, and put everything back
In its place and to pray three times a day.

Now I am relaxed about learning. My hair
Is cut short, like a soldier of World War Two,
All around, and my ears hold not just
My head but the whole sky.

And now they say about me: "You can rely on him."
That's where I've come! That's how low I've sunk!
Only those who truly love me
Know you can't.

Here, where a ruin wants to be
A new house again, its wish joins ours.
Even the thorns are weary of stinging, want to console.
A tombstone, ripped off a desecrated grave,
Was set in the new wall with its name and dates,
It is happy not to be forgotten.
And the children—only they could change it all—
Play between the rocks and the ruin.
They don't want to change a thing.

The cancellation of a love night in the Negev
Grows squills in the Jerusalem mountains.
Things are emptied and filled up.
A plant called sage doesn't soothe like a sage
But rips a deep wound in my forgetting,
Memory of an old thirst.

All are busy here with the art of remembering:
The ruin remembers, the orchard remembers,
The pit remembers its waters and the planted forest
Remembers on a marble plaque a distant holocaust
Or just the name of a dead donor
Who will be remembered a bit more than others.

But names are not important in these mountains,
As in a movie, where the names of the cast on the screen
Before the film don't yet matter, and after the film—
No more. The light goes on, the letters pale,
The wavy screen goes down, doors are opened and outside is night.

For in these mountains only summer and winter are important,
The dry and the wet, and people too
Are merely water reservoirs strewn everywhere,
Like wells and pits and underground springs.

A stewardess told us to extinguish all smoking materials
And did not detail, cigarette, cigar, or pipe.
I answered her in my heart: You have beautiful love material,
And I did not detail either.

And she told me to buckle up, bind myself
To the chair, and I answered her:
I want all the buckles in my life to have the shape of your mouth.

And she said: You want coffee now or later,
Or never. And she passed by me
Tall to the sky.

The small scar at the top of her arm
Testified that she will never be touched by smallpox
And her eyes testified that she'll never fall in love again:
She belongs to the conservative party
Of lovers of one great love in their life.

Flowers in a room are prettier than the seed's lust outside.
And though they are cut off from the earth
And without hope,
Their self-deluding desire adorns the room.
So you, sitting in my room, are beautiful
With love for someone else.

How can I help you.
The happy wear a thin necklace with black hair
And on their forehead the sign of joy.
And a Greek man looks with blue eyes
Into the dark thicket and is dreamed
By a distant woman, unknowingly.

I cannot help you
As I cannot help myself.

I too make square pictures
Out of round love
That knew no boundaries.

## → PEOPLE IN THE DARK ←
### ALWAYS SEE

People in the dark always see people
In the light. It's an old truth, since sun and night
Were created, people and darkness, and electricity.
A truth exploited by those who make war
For easy killing in an ambush, a truth that enables
The unhappy to see the happy, and the lonely—people in love
In a brightly lit room.

Yet true life is led between dark and light:
"I locked the door," you said,
An important sentence, full of destiny.
I still remember the words,
But I forgot on which side of the door they were said,
Inside or outside.

And from the only letter I wrote to you
I remember only the bitter taste of
The stamp's glue on my tongue.

## ❧ "HISTORY'S WINGS BEATING," ❧
## THEY USED TO SAY

Not far from the railroad tracks, near the painful Post Office,
I saw a tile plaque on an old house, and recognized the name of
The son of a man whose girl friend I took from him
Many years ago: she left him and came to me,
And this young man was born to another woman and didn't
Know about all that.

Those were days of great love and great destiny,
The foreign power imposed a curfew on the city and closed
Us for a sweet coupling in the room,
Guarded by well-armed soldiers.

For five shillings I changed the name of my forefathers
Of the Disapora into a proud Hebrew name matching hers.

That bitch ran off to America, got married to
A dealer in spices, pepper, cinnamon, cardamom,
And left me behind with my new name and the war.

"History's wings beating," as they used to say then, which
Almost killed me on the battlefield, blew
A pleasant breeze on her face in her safe place.

And in the wisdom of war they told me to put
My personal bandage above my heart,
The silly heart that still loved her
And the wise heart that will forget.

# SUFLAH SPRING IN THE JUDEAN MOUNTAINS

I took my two friends with me to find
The spring, that once, in days of dust and sorrow,
Quenched my thirst. Pipes took its waters
To orderly places, for fair distribution.
And the past years absorbed the smell of saturated plants
And the words that once described them
Now describe hard dead things.

Warning! Zone of longing!

It's so easy to be insane: if you just take
From the rememberer his memory,
From the landscape viewer the landscape
He observes, from the speaker his interlocutor,
And from the praying man his God.

We didn't find the spring
But at the end of the road we found
Strata of rest: the stone's rest
On the ground and the head's rest on the stone
And the sky's rest on this weary head.

Warning! Zone of longing!

## ✳ THERE ARE CANDLES ✴
## THAT REMEMBER

There are candles that remember for twenty-four hours,
As the label says. And there are candles that remember for eight hours.
And there are eternal candles that promise the memory of a man to his
    sons.

I am older than most buildings in this land and most of its forests
That are taller than me. And I'm still the child I was
Who carries a vessel full of precious fluid from one place
To another, and is careful, as in a dream, not to spill,
Fears punishment and hopes for a kiss if I get there.

Some of my father's friends still live in the city,
Scattered like antiquities, with no sign or explanation.

And my youngest daughter, in the year 2000
She'll be twenty-two. And her name is
Emanuella, may God be with us!

My soul is experienced and built, like terraces in the mountains
Against erosion. I'm the man who holds, I am
The mediator, the man-buckle.

# ➤ ON THE DAY MY DAUGHTER WAS BORN ⬅
## NOT A SINGLE PERSON DIED

On the day my daughter was born not a single person died
In the hospital and on the entrance gate
Was posted: "Today, cohens are permitted to enter."
The longest day of the year.
Overjoyed,
I drove with my friend to the hills of Sha'ar Ha-Gay.

We saw a pine tree sick and bare, just covered with an endless number of
pine cones. Tsvi said that trees about to die grow more cones than the liv-
ing one. And I told him: that was a poem and you didn't know it. Though
you are in the exact sciences, you made a poem. And he responded: and you,
though you are a dreamer, you made an exact girl with all the exact instru-
ments for her life.

# ✦ AGAIN, A LOVE IS FINISHED ✦

Again a love is finished, like a successful citrus season,
Or a digging season of archaeologists, bringing up from the depths
Exciting things that wanted to be forgotten.

Again a love is finished. As after the demolition
Of a big house, and the cleaning of the debris, you're standing
In the square empty lot, saying: How small
The space where the house stood
With all its stories and people.

And from the distant valley, you hear
A lonely tractor working,
And from the distant past, the clatter
Of a fork on a porcelain plate, mixing
And whipping up yoke with sugar for the child,
Clatter, clatter.

I dreamed a dream: seven fat, fleshy girls
Went out to the reeds, and I loved them in the reeds.
After them, seven thin girls, tanned by the east wind,
Went out and swallowed the fat ones with their starving thighs,
But their belly remained flat. I loved them too,
And they swallowed me too.

But the one who deciphered my dream,
The one I really loved,
Was both fat and thin, swallowing and swallowed.

And on the day after her I knew
I would never return to that place.

And in the spring after her they changed the flowers in the field
And the telephone directories with all the names.

And in the years after her a war broke out
And I knew I wouldn't dream any more dreams.

# JERUSALEM IS FULL
## OF USED JEWS

Jerusalem is full of Jews used up in history,
Secondhand Jews, slightly damaged, cheaper,
*And the eye looks to Zion* all the time. And all the eyes
Of the living and the dead break like eggs
At the edge of the bowl to make the city
Rich, fat, rising.

Jerusalem is full of tired Jews
And they're always being whipped again
Into memorial days and holidays,
Like bears dancing in the pain of their feet.

What does Jerusalem need? No mayor,
She needs a ringmaster, whip in hand,
To tame prophecies and train prophets to gallop
Around her in a circle, and teach her stones to form
A daring and dangerous order in the last act.

Afterward, they jump down to the ground
To the sound of applause and war.

*And the eye looks to Zion and cries.*

A girls goes out in the morning, like a knight—
Ponytail and riding motions.
Dresses, handbags, sunglasses, chain, buckles,
Like armor on her body.
But underneath all that
She's light and thin.

Sometimes she is naked at night and alone.
Sometimes she is naked and not alone.

You can hear the sound of bare feet
Fleeing: that was death.

And then, the sound of a kiss
Like the chirping of a night butterfly
Caught between two windows.

# ➤ PEACE OF MIND, ◆
## PEACE OF MIND


"Peace of mind," my parents said, "a person must
Reach peace of mind."
Like rich Arabs who spent their winters in Jericho
And summers in Ramallah and forgot the desert in between.
They too forget the middle. Or, as one moves
A sleeping child from the place it fell asleep to its bed
Without waking. Or like a man who planted a bomb
And gets away so he won't even hear the echo of his act.

A woman once told me: I live in peace
Outside history. And I told her: Rahab too said so,
"I dwell upon the wall," and see how
She entered history and did not get out of it.

Peace of mind, peace and mind. Just once I want to be
In the room I see every evening from my desk.
The curtain is always closed
And sometimes there's light inside.

I lived for quite a long time to wish
Just that, and not the kingdom of heaven.

As from *Thou shalt not seethe a kid in his mother's milk*
They made all the manifold laws of kashruth,
But the kid is forgotten and the milk is forgotten
And the mother is forgotten,

So, from *I love you*
We made all our life together.
But I did not forget you
As you were then.

Beautiful are the families of Jerusalem:
A mother from a Russian curse and a father from a Spanish curse,
A sister from an Arabic curse and brothers from the curses of the Torah
All sit together on the porch
On a summer day, in the perfume of jasmine.

Beautiful are the houses of Jerusalem:
All are mines whose time is set and no need
To be careful stepping on a threshold,
Turning a door knob, shaking a hand—
If their time hasn't come, there is no danger.

Yes,
Mister Detonator,
Mrs. Spring,
Boy Wick,
Girl Fuse,
Kids Delay,
And all the time sensitive, sensitive, sensitive.

The air above Jerusalem is filled with prayers and dreams
Like the air above cities with heavy industry.
Hard to breathe.

From time to time a new shipment of history arrives
And the buildings and towers are packing material,
Later discarded and piled up.

Sometimes candles arrive instead of people,
Then it's quiet.
And sometimes people instead of candles,
Then a commotion.

And in closed gardens, among jasmine bushes
Filled with fragrance, foreign consulates,
Like bad brides, jilted,
Waiting for their time.

They come here to visit the mourners.
They sit in Yad Va-Shem, wear grave faces at the Wailing Wall,
And laugh behind heavy curtains in hotel rooms.

They take pictures with the important dead at Rachel's Tomb
And at Herzl's Tomb and Ammunition Hill,
Weep for the beautiful heroism of our boys,
Lust for our tough girls,
And hang their underwear
For fast drying
In a blue, cold bathroom.

Once I sat on the stairs at the gate of David's Tower and put two heavy baskets next to me. A group of tourists stood there around their guide and I served as their orientation point. "You see that man with the baskets? A bit to the right of his head, there's an arch from the Roman period. A bit to the right of his head." But he moves, he moves!! I said to myself: redemption will come only when they are told: You see over there the arch from the Roman period? Never mind: but next to it, a bit to the left and lower, sits a man who bought fruit and vegetables for his home.

# YOU MUST NOT SHOW WEAKNESS

You must not show weakness
And you must be suntanned.
But sometimes I feel like the pale shawls
Of Jewish women, fainting
At weddings and on Yom Kippur.

You must not show weakness
And you must make a list
Of all the belongings you can load
On a baby carriage without babies.

The situation now is such
That if I pull the plug out of the bathtub
After a pleasant and indulgent bath,
I fear that all Jerusalem, and all the rest of the world
Will flow into the great darkness.

In the day, I set traps for my memories
And at night I work in Balaam's enterprises,
Turning a curse into a blessing and a blessing into a curse.

And you must not show weakness.
Sometimes I collapse inside myself,
Imperceptibly. I'm a two-legged ambulance,
Carrying the collapsed man inside me, shaking
On his way to Zero Aid.
I sound a wailing siren
And people think it's normal speech.

Straight from prejudice you leaped to me,
Hardly had any time to get dressed.

I want to Jewify you with my circumcised body,
I want to wrap you in tefillin straps from head to foot.

I want to dress you in gold and velvet,
Like a Torah Scroll, and hang a Magen David on your neck

And kiss your thighs
Like a mezuzah on the doorpost.

I shall teach you the old custom of washing
Feet with love:

I washed my own memories,
I wore them a lot and grew tired.

And my eyes grew tired of the square letters of my language,
I want letters flowing like your body.

With you, I don't want to feel like a prophet of rage
Or a prophet of consolation.

I almost
Succeeded:

But when you cried, the tears in your eyes gleamed
Like snow and Christmas ornaments.

Two girls live in the old house.
Sometimes they overflow, sometimes
They disappear like the torrents in the Negev,
Sometimes they are ten, sometimes only one.

Sometimes their yellow light is on all night
As in a chicken coop, for twenty-four hours
Of love, sometimes just a small reddish light
Like a candy with a saint's halo around it.

And a big mulberry tree stands in the middle of their yard.
In the spring, plenty of fruit on the tree, and a lot
On the ground.

One bends to gather it,
The other stretches to pick it.
My eyes enjoy both:
One wears only a man's undershirt, nothing more,
The other, sandals with laces
Winding almost to her navel.

If my belly aches,
I feel like the whole round globe.
If I have a headache,
My laughter laughs in the wrong place in my body.
And if I cry, they're putting my father in his grave
Into earth too large, he won't grow into it.
And if I'm a porcupine, I'm an inverted porcupine,
The thorns grow inward, to hurt.
And if I am the prophet Ezekiel, I see in the vision of the chariot
Only bull's legs filled with dung and filthy wheels.

I'm like a porter carrying a big, heavy lounge chair
On his back to a distant place
Without knowing that you can lower it to the ground and sit in it.

I'm like a machine gun, somewhat old-fashioned
But very precise: when I love,
The recoil is very strong, all the way back to childhood, and it hurts.

And the land is divided into districts of memory and provinces of hope,
And its inhabitants blend with each other
As people returning from a wedding merge with those returning from a
  funeral.

And the land is not divided into zones of war and zones of peace.
And a man digging a foxhole against shells
Will return and lie there with his girl,
If he lives to see peace.

And the land is beautiful.
Even enemies all around adorn it
With their weapons shining in the sun
Like beads on a neck.

And the land is a package land:
She is neatly wrapped, everything inside, well tied
And the strings sometimes hurt.

And the land is very small,
I can encompass it inside me.
The erosion of the ground erodes my rest, too,
And the level of Lake Kineret is always on my mind.
Hence, I can feel all of it
With my eyes closed: sea-valley-mountain.
Hence, I can remember all that happened in her
All at once, like a person remembering
His whole life in the moment of dying.

# GREAT CALM: QUESTIONS
## AND ANSWERS

People in the hall lighted so it hurts
Spoke about religion
In the life of contemporary people
And about the place of God.

People spoke in excited voices
As at airports.
I left them:
I opened an iron door with the sign
"Emergency" and entered
A great calm: questions and answers.

# An Hour of Grace

✢ ✢ ✢ ✢ ✦ ✦ ✦ ✦

1983

I once thought it could be resolved like this:
People gather at a bus-stop at midnight
For the last bus that won't come,
First a few, then more and more.
It was a chance to be close to each other,
To change everything and start together a new world.

But they dispersed.
(The hour of grace passed with no return.)
Each will go his own way
Each will be a domino
With one side open
To find a new correspondent
In games that never end.

"Among the stars you may be right,
But not here," in mid-speech
You shifted to quiet weeping as one shifts
In the middle of a letter from blue to black
When the ink dries out, or as they used to
Change horses on a long trip:
The speech got tired, the tears are fresh.

Summer seeds fluttered into the room.
In the window, an almond tree turning black.
It too a valiant fighter in the eternal war
Between sweet and bitter.

Look, as time is not in watches
Love is not in bodies,
Bodies only display love.

But we shall remember this evening
As a person remembers the motions of swimming
From one summer to the next. "Among the stars
You may be right, but not here."

# THE REAL HERO OF THE
## SACRIFICE OF ISAAC

The real hero of the sacrifice was the ram
Who had no idea about the conspiracy of the others.
He apparently volunteered to die in place of Isaac.
I want to sing a memorial song about the ram,
His curly wool and human eyes,
The horns, so calm in his living head.
When he was slaughtered they made *shofars* of them,
To sound the blast of their war
Or the blast of their coarse joy.

I want to remember the last picture
Like a beautiful photo in an exquisite fashion magazine:
The tanned, spoiled youngster all spiffed up,
And beside him the angel, clad in a long silk gown
For a formal reception.
Both with hollow eyes
Observe two hollow places,

And behind them, as a colored background, the ram
Grasping the thicket before the slaughter.

The angel went home
Isaac went home
And Abraham and God left much earlier.

But the real hero of the sacrifice
Is the ram.

# THE SAME EMBROIDERY,
## THE SAME PATTERN

I saw a man wearing a skullcap embroidered
With the pattern of the underwear
Of a woman I loved
A long time ago.

He didn't understand why I looked at him
And why I turned back after he passed,
He shrugged his shoulders and went away.

And I mumbled to myself: the same
Colors, the same embroidery, the same pattern,
The same embroidery, the same pattern.

She poured herbal tea to soothe
His mood. She said: "Your wishes
Are passions tamed in the course of millennia,
You know, like wolves and dogs.
Tonight you'll be like thousands of years ago."

She led him by his rasping prick
To a white bedroom, to please
The eyes of God and the eyes of men.

"You'd be surprised what can become
Wings. You'd be surprised; even
Heavy thighs, even memories."

She took off her long dress,
The external soul of her body.
The internal one she left intact.

To erase the expression of coarse lust
On my face, I think about the problems of the world,
Wars, police states, and such.
I fight oppression and injustice everywhere,
But actually I want to fight
Only for beautiful women,
Poor and rich, exploited and exploiting, all of them.

(I know a man who joined a protest movement
Only because there were a lot of young women in it.)

In totalitarian regimes, the women's
Cunts are particularly big and their appetites endless.
The men, on the other hand, their erections are small and quick.
In a Czech photo I saw two young women
Sitting at a big window in a café:
One—her face, a white blot left by the censor in a newspaper,
The other—a bartered bride.

But under their skirts they wear
Tiny, delicate panties,
Smuggled in from countries of freedom.

A woman dealing with matters of the past
Is in bed with a man who does things of the present.
A sorceress and an owner of modern vehicles.

Her white dress hangs on a string on the porch
And cools the hot night.
Next to her, his colorful shirt, sleeves drooping,
Still dripping, praying upside down.

Together, they exercise a long lovemaking
As reparation for everything.
All their forefathers dreamed of doing
They do to each other,
A lot from behind, a lot like animals.

At midnight, comes the bearded voyeur,
Peeps through the shutters,
Perhaps he's one of the latest prophets
Collecting material for his visions.

Mark them with signs. Remember the clothes
Worn by a person you love,
So on the day of loss you'll be able to say: last seen
Dressed in such and such, a brown coat, a white hat.
Mark them with signs. For they have no face
And their soul is hidden and their weeping is like their laughter
And their silence and their scream rise to the same height
And the heat of the bodies is between 97 and 104 degrees
And they have no life outside this narrow gap,
And they have no statue or image or memory
And they have paper cups at their celebrations
And paper plates to use only one time.

Mark them with signs. For the world
Is full of people torn from their sleep
And there is no one to mend the tear,
And not like wild animals, they live
Each in his lonely lair and they die
Together on battlefields
And in hospitals.
And the earth will swallow them all,
The good and the bad together, like Korah's tribe,
All of them rebelling against death
With open mouths to the last minute
And praise and curse are one
Lament. Mark, mark them with signs.

A man in his life has no time to have
Time for everything.
He has no room to have room
For every desire. Ecclesiastes was wrong to claim that.

A man has to hate and love all at once,
With the same eyes to cry and to laugh
With the same hands to throw stones
And to gather them,
Make love in war and war in love.

And hate and forgive and remember and forget
And order and confuse and eat and digest
What long history does
In so many years.

A man in his life has no time.
When he loses he seeks
When he finds he forgets
When he forgets he loves
When he loves he begins forgetting.

And his soul is knowing
And very professional,
Only his body remains an amateur
Always. It tries and fumbles.
He doesn't learn and gets confused,
Drunk and blind in his pleasures and pains.

In autumn, he will die like a fig,
Shriveled, sweet, full of himself.
The leaves dry out on the ground,
And the naked branches point
To the place where there is time for everything.

I saw a modern girl and understood
The big mistake of resurrection:
People who die, others rise in their place.

A modern girl, under her dress
She wears a short leotard,
And under the leotard, an even shorter
Bikini: she is always ready for everything,

And her eyes are shortsighted,
The only eyes good for this time.
I think it's a terrible time
And she thinks it's wonderful.

Modern girl, come live in my generation,
Or at least toss some
Strange words into me, like coins
Into a pool, for good luck.
At the bottom, they will always be seen clearly,
I shall not touch them.
No one will touch them.

# THE AGED PARENTS

The aged parents visited their aging son.
He prepared for the visit. The night before he dreamed.
On his face no trace of tears, on his body no trace of blood.
Dried semen on his belly
For he's of a generation of love.

The parents visited their son. They sit
Crowded and huddled as at a parents' meeting
In school, on the small, narrow bench
Of a classroom.

He's tired, he's an old fetus.
He's empty like a fat telephone directory.

Now you hear the whistle of empty testes,
A dog wails, *The 9th of Av.*

A chill rises from the ground,
He hasn't said the *Shema* in a long time.

A hard egg, symbol of mourning and ash
And also a memory of a school outing.

The aged parents visited their aging son.
Had he fallen in one of the wars
He'd have saved them and himself
A lot of shame and grief.

I was born in 1924. If I were a violin my age
I wouldn't be very good. As a wine I would be splendid
Or altogether sour. As a dog I would be dead. As a book
I would begin to be expensive or thrown out by now.
As a forest I would be young, as a machine ridiculous,
And as a human being I'm very tired.

I was born in 1924. When I think about humanity
I think just about those born in my year.
Their mothers gave birth with my mother,
Wherever they were, in hospitals or in dark flats.

On this day, my birthday, I would like
To say a great prayer for you,
Whose load of hopes and disappointments
Pulls your life downward,
Whose deeds diminish
And whose gods increase,
You are all brothers of my hope and companions of my despair.

May you find the right rest,
The living in their life, the dead in their death.

He who remembers his childhood better
Than others is the winner,
If there are any winners at all.

On these low hills, a life meant to go on a long time
Came to an end. What we thought was smoke
Turned out to be more solid than ephemeral life.
Even the abandoned drilling wells turned into part
Of the beautiful landscape, reminders of places of love and death
Like the trees and water towers.

This winter, the torrent ripped into the almond grove,
Tore off chunks, exposing the tree roots,
Beautiful in the sun like branches,
For only a few days.

Here, the sand transmits to the limestone
And the limestone to the light earth and the light
Earth to the heavy, and the heavy earth to the rocks
At the edge of the plain. Tradition and continuity,
Transmission and change without people,
Plenty and paucity. And the buzz of bees
And the buzz of time are one.

(In Kibbutz Gvar-'am, in a wooden shed, I once saw
The books of Buber and Rilke in a simple bookcase
And reproductions of Van Gogh and Modigliani
On the wall, on the eve of battles and death.)

There is also a grove of eucalyptus trees,
Pale as people sick with longing.
They do not know what they long for
And I tell them in a quiet
Voice: Australia, Australia.

If my parents and your parents
Had not immigrated to Israel
In 1936,
We would have met in 1944
On the ramp in Auschwitz.
I at 20,
You at 5.

Where's *mame*?
Where's *tate*?

What's your name?
*Channa'le*.

# THE LAST WORD
## IS CAPTAIN

My head didn't grow anymore
When I stopped growing,
But the memories multiplied,
So, I must assume they are now in my belly,
My thighs and my legs. A walking archive,
An ordered disorder, a storage room weighing down
An overloaded ship.

Sometimes I want to lie on a bench in a park:
It would have changed my status
From lost inside to lost outside.

Words begin to abandon me
Like rats from a sinking ship.
The last word is captain.

What entanglement in this small country,
What confusion! "The second son of the first husband
Goes out to his third war, the Second Temple
Of the first God gets destroyed every year."
My doctor treats the guts
Of the cobbler who repairs the shoes of the man
Who defended me in my fourth trial.
In my comb strange hair, in my handkerchief strange sweat,
Memories of others stick to me
Like dogs to the smell,
And I must drive them off
Scolding, with a stick.

All are contaminated by each other,
All touch each other,
Leave fingerprints, and the Angel of Death
Must be an expert detective
To tell them apart.

I once knew a soldier who fell in the war,
Three or four women mourned him:
He loved me. I loved him.
He was mine. I was his.

The Soltam Co. makes both pots and mortars
And I do not make anything.

# ➤ THE WONDERFUL BAKER ✦

I sat on the wide sidewalk of Café Willheim in Ramatayim
In the morning hours.
The folding chairs and folding tables
Witnessed life with no permanence.
The heavy trucks passing by on the highway
Shook up old memories.

A man needs so little to cry,
Some shaking, some remembering, some pain, and some water
From the water used to irrigate the citrus groves,
From the plenty of water that won't put out love.

They posted obituaries
On the trunk of the thick tree,
The golden glue still drips like sap
And the name of the newly deceased gleams in the sun.
His name was the name of a city from that world in Europe.
How few are the people whose last name
Is the name of the place where they were born or live
Or die. History flows on lazily,
Sticky as lava from distant eruptions.
A child in Elath is named Abraham from Mesopotamia
And a dead man in Ramatayim is named after a distant city
He never saw in his life.

Most of our lives we are busy with the dead.
We close their eyes, wind them in sheets,
Mourn them and remember them,
Live in a house built by the dead,
Read a book written by the dead,
Live by laws enacted by the dead in their lifetime
And remember their memories.

I sit in a café on the highway
And eat filled cakes, soul cakes for all the living.

Oh, wonderful baker at your oven,
You're more advanced than all the scientists,
For you know that body and soul are one
And a vessel and its contents are one
And a cake and its filling are one,
As a man and his death are one.

There is a street where they sell only red meat
And there is a street where they sell only clothes and perfumes.

And there is a day when I see only beautiful youths
And there is a day when I see only cripples and the blind
And those covered with leprosy and spastics and those with twisted lips.

Here they build a house and there they destroy
Here they dig into the earth
And there they dig into the sky,
Here they sit and there they walk
Here they hate and there they love.

But he who loves Jerusalem
By the tourist book or the prayer book
Is like one who loves a woman
By a manual of sex positions.

# THE SWEET VOICE
## FROM THE KIBBUTZ

They put me in a small, clean room
In a long house, covered with vines.
I lay on my back and thought
About the courage of plants to climb
And the weariness of man to go on
And his weariness to stay still.

And at midnight I heard a sweet voice under my window:
The sweet voice entered the room next to mine
The sweet voice closed the door
The sweet voice stripped naked
The sweet voice read a book
The sweet voice turned off the light
The sweet voice got up early in the morning
The sweet voice left
And some time later I left too
And shall not see the sweet voice.
But to the end of my life, I shall never stop wishing
*To see the voices.*

A precise woman with a short haircut makes order
In my thoughts and drawers,
A woman moves feelings around like furniture
Into a new order.
A woman with a body tied up and divided
Between above and below,
A woman with the eyes of a weather forecast,
Unbreakable glass,
Even her passionate screams are ordered
One after the other, not intermingled:
Domestic dove, then wild dove,
Then a peacock, a wounded peacock, peacock, peacock.
Then a wild dove, domestic dove, dove, dove
Owl, owl, owl.

A precise woman: on the rug by the bed
Her shoes always point away from the bed.
(My shoes point toward it.)

Hamadiya, memory of bliss. The forties
And love in the barn. The chaff still pricks me even though
My body has washed countless times since then and my clothes
Have been changed and changed and the girl left into
The fifties and disappeared in the sixties and was lost for good
In the seventies—the chaff still pricks me,
My throat is sore from shouting:
Come back again you
Come back to me come back time come back jujube!

Love was the raw material of this poor country,
Reality and dream joined to make the weather
And joy and sadness were still
Aspects of the climate in these places.
The dangers were beating around us like the throbbing
Of wells hidden in the orchards
And the voice that began then as a voice
Calling for help, turned into calm singing.

And we didn't know then that remnants of happiness
Are like remnants of every collapse
That you have to clear away to start anew.

# From Man You Came
# and to Man
# You Shall Return

❖·❖·❖·❖ ❖·❖·❖·❖

## 1989

### My Mother's Death and the Lost Battles
### for the Future of Her Children

My mother white on her bed in the world
Like the black stain
Of a bonfire once in a field.

On the dresser the comb
That combed her hair
To the side
Of her passing days
And left her forehead bare
On the pillow.

And outside,
The lost battles for the future of her children.

### Oh, Ivy Growing

Oh, ivy growing on the wall of the room
Of a dying woman. Growing too
Is slow dying, rising up from below.

Oh, last gazes of a living person,
Like flies around a lamp on a summer evening.
And all the gazes end in light
And all walking ends in dance,
And all speaking ends in song
And all silence ends in eternity.

And my mother died at night. Quietly
She lay in the dark, closed and arranged
For the next day, like a dining hall
Closed and arranged, tables already set
For others' breakfast.


## My Mother on Her Sickbed

My mother on her sickbed with the lightness and hollowness of a person
Who has already said goodbye at an airport
In the beautiful and quiet area
Between parting and takeoff.

My mother on her sickbed.
All she had in her life is now
Like empty bottles in front of the door
That will show once more with colored labels
What filled them with joy and sadness.

Her last words, "Take the flowers out of the room,"
She said seven days before her death,
Then she closed herself for seven days,
Like the seven days of mourning.

But even her death created in her room
A warm hominess
With her sleeping face and the cup with its teaspoon
And the towel and the book and the glasses,
And her hand on the blanket, the same
Hand that felt my forehead, in childhood.


## Now She Breathes

Now she breathes quietly, I said. No, now
She screams inside in great pain, said the doctor. He

Asked my permission to remove the wedding ring from her finger,
For it was so swollen. I gave permission in the name of the pain and in the
    name
Of my father who never left her in his life. We turned
The ring like a magic ring from stories, but
It did not come off and no miracle occurred. The doctor asked
Permission to cut the ring, and he cut it with the delicacy
Of cautious tweezers.

Now she laughs, she is training for the laughter of there.
Now she cries, she is weaning from the crying of here.

Her passport photo was taken many, many years
Ago. She never went abroad since she immigrated
To Eretz-Israel. The death certificate
Needs no picture.

## And My Mother from the Times

And my mother from the times when they painted
Marvelous fruit on silver bowls and made do with that,
And people sailed through their lives
Like ships, with the wind or against it,
True to their destination.

I ask myself what is better:
A man dying old or a man dying young?
As if asking what weighs less
A pound of feathers or a pound of iron.

I want feathers, feathers, feathers.

## My Mother Died on Shavuot

My mother died on Shavuot when they finished counting the Omer,
Her oldest brother died in 1916, fallen in the war,

I almost fell in 1948,
And my mother died in 1983.
Everyone dies at the end of some counting,
Long or short,
Everyone falls in a war,
They all deserve a wreath and a ceremony and an official letter.
When I stand at my mother's grave
It's like saluting
And the hard words of the Kaddish a salvo
Into the summer skies.

We buried her in Sanhedria next to my father's grave,
We kept the place for her
As in a bus or cinema:
Leaving flowers and stones so no one would take her place.

(Twenty years ago this graveyard was
On the border, facing the enemy's positions.
The tombstones were a good defense against tanks.)

But in my childhood there was a botanical garden here
Lots of flowers with frail wooden tags
Bearing names of flowers in Hebrew and Latin:
Common Rose, Mediterranean Sage,
Common Scream, Tufted Weeping,
Annual Weeping, Perennial Mourning,
Red Forget-Me-Not, Fragrant Forget-Me-Not,
Forget-me-not, forget.


*The Body Is the Cause of Love*

The body is the cause of love,
Later, the fortress guarding it,
Later, the prison of love.
But when the body dies, love emerges free
And in great abundance,

Like a broken slot machine played for luck,
And pours all at once,
With a roaring ring, all the coins
Of generations of luck.

### Free

She is free. Free from the body
And free from the soul and from the blood that is the soul,
Free from wishes and from sudden fear
And from fear for me, free from honor and from shame
Free from hope and from despair and from fire and from water,
Free from the color of her eyes and from the color of her hair,
Free from furniture and free from knife spoon fork,
Free from the heavenly Jerusalem and from the earthly Jerusalem,
Free from identity and from identity documents,
Free from round seals
And from square seals,
Free from photos and free from clips,
She is free.

And all the letters and all the numbers
That arranged her life are free too
For new combinations and new destinies and new games
Of all the generations that will come after her.

### Now She Descends

Now she descends into the earth,
Now she is on a level with the telephone cables, electrical wires,
Pure water pipes and impure water pipes,
Now she descends to deeper places,
Deeper than deep, there lie
The reasons for all this flowing,
Now she is in the layers of stone and ground water,
There lie the motives of wars and the movers of history
And the future destinies of nations and peoples

Yet unborn:
My mother, Satellite of Redemption,
Turns the earth
Into real heavens.

After everything I do, they march
As at funerals: the child I was years ago,
The boy in his first love I was, the soldier I was
In those days, the gray-haired man I was an hour ago,
And others, strangers too, that I was and forgot,
One of them may be a woman.

And all together with moving, remembering lips
And all together with damp, shining eyes
And all says words of eulogy and consolation
And all will turn back again to their affairs and their times,
As at funerals.

And one said to his friend: "The main task
In modern industry is to create materials
That are stronger and lighter."
So he said and cried, and went his way,
As at funerals.

Carrots grow happily into the earth,
A slaughtered lamb's head in the butcher shop inspires calm in me,
Half-sweet wine
Seeks its bitter half
And I'm in trouble.

The flute seller plays to sell his flutes
The drum seller drums
The whore bares her thighs
And I'm in great trouble.

Fruits are drawn on the door of the fruit store,
Fish are drawn on the fish restaurant,
A young man is drawn on the entrance to the war,
And I'm in great trouble.

From a man who loses,
I turned into a man lost,
I am tired of doors,
I want windows, just windows,
I want clothes
That would be light and loose on my body,
Like hands waving goodbye, with no pain.
I'm afraid of what the past
Will do to my future.
And from the synagogue of my childhood
Only the skies remained
Which I saw then from the windows.
God, I'm in great trouble.

Human bodies are different from each other
But their souls are alike, full of brilliant utility,
Like airports.
Do not give me your soul,
Give me your body which I shall never know to the full,
Give me the vessel and not its contents.

Stand with me in airports
Where the pain of parting is dressed up
In pretty words, like orphans,
Where drinks and food are expensive
But people and their destinies cheap.

A man talks into a telephone
And his mouth drinks sorrow and love from the receiver.

Even those who cry have
Hands white as brides,
Arms free from embracing,
What will they do in the world?

Let my soul die with my body.

Because of love and because of making love
And because the pain of the unborn
Is greater than the pain of the born,
I said to the woman: "Let us make a man
In our own image." And we did. But he grows
Different from us,
Day by day.

Furtively he eavesdrops on his parents' talk,
He doesn't understand but he grows on those words,
As a plant grows without understanding
Oxygen, nitrogen, and other elements.

Later on he stands before the opened
Holy Arks of legend
And before the lighted display windows
Of history, the Maccabean wars, David and Goliath,
The suicides of Masada, the ghetto uprising,
Hannah and her seven sons,
He stands with gaping eyes
And, deep down, he grows a vow like a big flower:
To live, to live, not to die like them.

When he writes, he starts the letters from the bottom.
When he draws two fighting knights
He starts with the swords, then come the hands,
And then the head. And outside the page
And beyond the table—hope and peace.

Once he did something bad in school
And was punished: I saw him,
Alone in an empty classroom,
Eating with the gestures of a tamed beast.
I told him, fight me
But he fights the school,

Law and order.
I told him, pour out your wrath on me
But he caresses me and I caress him.

The first real
Big school outing
Is the outing from which
They never return.

You visit me in an apple.
We listen together to the knife
Paring all around us, carefully
Not to tear the peel.

You speak to me, I can trust your voice,
It holds pieces of hard pain
As real honey holds waxen pieces
Of honeycomb.

With my fingers I touch your lips.
This too is a gesture of prophecy.
Your lips are red, as a scorched field is black.
Everything comes true.

You visit me in an apple.
And you stay with me in the apple
Till the paring knife finishes its work.

I cannot imagine
How we shall live without each other,
So we said.

And since then we live inside that image,
Day after day, far from each other,
Far from the house
Where we said those words.

Every time a door closes, a window opens,
As under anesthesia, no pain.

Pains come later.

# MEMORY OF LOVE—
## TERMS AND CONDITIONS

We were like children who didn't want to
Come out of the sea. And the blue night came
And then the black night.

What did we bring back for the rest of our lives,
A flaming face, like the burning bush
That won't consume itself till the end of our lives.

We made a strange arrangement between us:
If you come to me, I'll come to you,
Strange terms and conditions: If you forget me,
I'll forget you.
Strange terms and lovely things.

The ugly things we had to do
For the rest of our lives.

# ELECAMPANE, JASMINE, VINE, AND OLEANDER

Elecampane has no hope, but it has a connection
To hope and a sharp smell
Of the lust of the living and the dead.
Elecampane grows only near human dwellings,
Even near dwellings razed to the ground,
Proud concubine of ruins that never betrayed,
Memory whore, holy harlot of a burned temple,
Keeper of libido that won't forget a thing,
Mourning woman strong as death,
Dog on a grave, the last of the faithful,
Eternal light.

Jasmine covers all. Its fragrance and courage
Fill the world, like thunder,
Its white flowers witness the darkness of our life
And its smell degenerate and sweet.
Jasmine is a tree, not a climbing bush,
It screams, I am not a climbing bush,
I am a tree among trees.
The world is full of such screams
About such mistakes that will never be righted.

A vine is a home, a man too is a home,
A vine sleeps like a child,
One hand on his cheek, and the other hand
Stretched out beyond his sleep.

Refusals add sweetness to the world:
The child's refusal to be a man,
The grape's refusal to die bitter.

Oleanders love to grow
In abandoned railroad stations,
Their meeting places with the elecampane

And the jasmine and the vine, climbing
In vain, on walls with no roof,
But they have skies and they have God.

Last summer I walked on the abandoned railroad tracks
From Akhziv to Rosh Ha-Nikra,
I went instead of the train that doesn't go here anymore.
Forty years the tracks were silent,
The cadence of my walk from tie to tie
Calmed my legs and my legs calmed
What will never be calmed.

## MEMORY OF LOVE—
## OPENING THE WILL

I'm still inside the room. Two days from now
I will see it from the outside only,
The closed shutter of your room where we loved one another
And not all mankind.

And we shall turn to our new lives
In the special way of careful preparations
For death, turning to the wall
As in the Bible.

The God above the air we breathe,
The God who made us two eyes and two legs
Made us two souls too.

And we shall open these days
On a day far away from here, as one opens
The will
Years after a death.

Death in war begins
With one young man
Descending the stairs.

Death in war begins
With closing a door in silence,
Death in war begins
With opening a window to see.

Hence, do not weep for the one who goes,
Weep for the one who descends the stairs of his house,
Weep for the one who puts his last key
In his back pocket.
Weep for the picture that remembers instead of us,
Weep for the paper that remembers,
Weep for the tears that do not remember.

And in this spring,
Who will stand up and say to the dust:
From man you came and to man you shall return.

Pleas stuck in the cracks of the Wailing Wall,
Crumpled, wadded notes.

Somewhere else, a note stuck in an old iron gate
Half hidden in a jasmine bush:
"I just couldn't come,
Hope you'll understand."

Toward the end of the war, I brought from the Negev to the wine cellar
The last military kit bag of Itzhak from Rishon Le-Zion.
For the line of defense of the wine cellar passed through the Negev
Where he fell. I brought the kit bag to his father, a veteran wine cellar
    man,
For I was told not to go to the women's house, to mother and sister,
But to the man's place, to the father. In a rubber apron
Up to his chin and rubber boots up to his knees
He stood in the fermenting of the wine and the raging of his life.
He called his colleagues from between the barrels,
In a loud voice in the dark cellar:
Here is his friend who was with him when he died,
Here is his last kit bag, here is the towel,
The big striped towel we gave him on his way to Negev.

Oh, Itzhak, you fell in the Negev
And your father cries in a wine cellar.
I remember the silly song
By Ibn-Gabirol: "At the end of the wine, The eye of mine,
Runs streams of water, Streams of water." Here,
The wine did not end, but the eyes ran out of tears.

In the cellar's ceiling, yellow lamps burned
In cages, like trapped souls,
And in the big, dark barrels
The fermentation began that will never cease.

# ❧ EVIDENCE ❧

An abandoned tractor sinking in the mud,
A shirt tossed on the seat, crushed grass
Are evidence of a great love, a bit further down
Between the thick bushes, oleander and reeds.
Evidence is always more abundant than necessary.
I think of the things people buy
In stores in various combinations,
I saw soap, matches, and two potatoes
In one basket and other things
That don't belong together.

I think of history's effort
To bring things together and to remember
And of the loneliness of one ancient jug
In the museum, standing in a glass cabinet
Especially illuminated, shadowed from forgetting
And barred from death. I think of the basalt rocks
In the old Roman bridge, those too
Are evidence for things I do not know.

Round time and square time
Both pass with the same speed,
Only the sound is different in their passing.
And many memorial candles together
Make a big light of joy.

I passed by an imposing house with a sign saying:
"Language School," and I called out: my Lord,
From-the-depths I called my Lord. For people
Call their God, and their God calls only
Other Gods. One bird calls to another bird,
Only water sometimes talks in voices
Of people at swimming pools in the summer.

Language school. Here languages learn how
To get used to foreign lips, to a dark palate,
To a laughing mouth and a crying mouth.
Languages learn and will never end,
Like yearnings.

This life gets ever harder,
But the response to it grows ever softer,
Like a ball coming back from the wall
Where it was hurled in rage
And its bounces are appeased and soft
Until it rests and is mute.

And one woman said to a crying child,
"Don't cry, a nice boy doesn't cry."
I heard this as I walked by
The "Language School,"
And called out: my Lord, from-the-depths.

I have to pay an entrance fee
For the place where I have memories
Of wonderful things that happened in the past:
This is the distance of time, this is the love
Of homeland, this is my life.

Cascade of joy into a pool of sadness,
So simple: sound and foam.
And the big stone where we made our bonfire
Stayed black, so it remembers
And this is the color of its remembering.

So I threw away the entrance ticket
And called the place: Rooms.

A rosebush hangs over the wall, witness to bliss
Of others, in closed gardens that break your heart
With so much yearning,
Plenty and loss, like the last bread
Tossed over the wall of a besieged city,
A sweet seized moment in red ardor
On the faces of prophets of the End of Days,
Death and lust, sleep of the waking, talk
In a dream, and time in vain. A rosebush covers
A letterbox holding the letter of pain:
Between the event at the window
And the event at the door
Sometimes a whole life passes.

A rosebush over the wall.
I know a scholar of hard history
Who sired three soft daughters,
Beauties who grew up and left home.
But a rosebush hangs over the wall.

# ✤ SANDALS ✤

Sandals are the skeleton of a full shoe,
And its only soul.
Sandals are the reins of my galloping feet
And the tefillin straps of my weary, praying leg.

Sandals are the stretch of private soil
I tread on wherever I go,
Representatives of my homeland, my true country.
The sky of small fry swarming underneath,
The day of their coming destruction.

Sandals are the youth of the shoe,
The trace of its trek to the desert.

I don't know when they'll lose me
Or when I'll lose them, but they will be lost
Each in another place:
One near my house,
Between rocks and small bushes,
The other will sink in the sand
Near the great sea,
Like the sun setting
Like the sun setting.

The land is plowed up. Inside is outside,
Like a person who confessed.

And all the crumbling things
Are on their way to being one again,
Like the "One" drawn out in a loud voice
At the end of *Shema Israel*.

My children in Jerusalem
Turn in their sleep in the direction of my travels,
Into the past or into the future.

Empty rivers think I am water,
A cloud, a shadow of a cloud,
And I think, an empty riverbed.

I was left with two friends:
A geologist and a biologist.
The territory between them is mine.

Dangerous country. Full of suspect objects
And booby-trapped people. Everything can be
The beginning of a new religion: every birth, death,
Conflagration of thorns in a field, smoke.
Even lovers must be careful in their deeds and words,
Arms stretched for an embrace, whisper at midnight,
Secret crying, a distant gaze, descending a staircase
In a white dress. All those are the beginning of a new religion.

Even the migrating birds know it,
They come in spring or in autumn and do not stay,
Like the gods of this country that never stay.
And he who says here it was is a prophet of consolation,
And he who says here it will be is a prophet of rage.

And from north to south, summer joy has no end,
And the warnings against deep and stormy waters
And the warnings against a drought above ground,
And memorial tombstones everywhere, are weights
To keep the history of the country from flying off
Like papers in the wind.

I sit in the waiting room with bridegrooms many years
Younger than me. Had I lived in ancient days,
I would be a prophet. But now I wait quietly
To register my name and the name of my beloved in the big Book
Of Marriages and to answer questions I can still
Answer. I filled my life with words,
I gathered in my body information that can feed the
Intelligence services of several countries.

With heavy steps I carry light thoughts,
As in my youth I carried thoughts heavy with destiny
On light feet, almost dancing with so much future.

The pressure of my life brings my birthday closer
To my death day, like history books,
Where the pressure of history brings those two
Numbers together with the name of a dead king,
Just a hyphen separating them.

I hold on to the hyphen with all my being,
As to a life raft, I live on it,
And the oath not to be alone is on my lips,
The *voice of the bridegroom* and the *voice of the bride* and the voice
Of children playing in the streets of Jerusalem
And in the mountains of Yehuda.

Claudia is a multitude of Jews
Made into one pretty girl in Mexico.
Veronica a multitude of rumors.

I'd like to describe them as in travel accounts
Of the last century
With a lot of love and little knowledge.

I don't know what words make them happy,
What words make them sad,
What are their vistas of despair and their vistas of hope,
Deep plantations and deserts,
Distant snow-capped mountains,
And what does night bring.

Claudia is pretty, like windows open to the sea,
She is a scout to the lands of separation.
Veronica is Trotsky's great-granddaughter,
Her lovely hair covers the wound in her grandfather's skull.
She lives in a house with a lot of books and a lot of death.

Lately I saw them together in the holy
Ceremony of picture-taking at the foot of the stairs
Among people, who clustered and scattered
And the trumpet that was summoned to soothe
Opened memories, old and painful.

Claudia will carry on her shoulders
Her fading face.
Veronica will take with her
All the words I didn't know.
My soul will throb for them
Like the skin of a dozing dog.
The hand and the handle both lost.
And the bee drowned in its own honey.

People travel all day long
To sleep in another place. Who will measure
Their distances and who will carry their voice,
And if, where will he carry it?

Only while traveling do people open up,
Like banners that open only in the wind
To show what they are,
Stars and sun, stripes and circles,
Sadness and joy in the splendor of their destiny
And in all colors of memory.

I sit in the moving train,
My eyes fall in love hastily
With all they see along the way:
A plow stuck in the soil passes by,
High tanks filled with water and gasoline,
And other transfusions for the transients to their death,
And branches of trees bend and rise,
This too is a lesson, a great lesson in everything,
And the beat beats like a brutal butcher.

My internal world is insured and valuable,
And my private life will not make a scratch,
Won't leave a trace on all
That is passing by the traveling window.

Now I open the newspaper,
World events move with me,
The travel makes them light.
I see a picture of a little girl
Lost two or three months ago.
In the picture she is smiling,
In the world she is lost.

Do I think of the children of my children, yet unborn?
What is the length of my arms into their future,
How far will my voice reach, calling them
To come home from their play?

What is the area of womb protection,
The span of body heat,
The range of feelings, the private domain of hope?
What are the courtyards of love,
The defended preserve of worry,
The territorial waters of fear?
And where is the absent horizon of generations to come,
And the border of eternity of my grandchildren's grandchildren?

The paper fell from my hand. We pass by
A splendid white house in a big garden,
Slowly enough to see
The bliss among the tall trees
And fast enough not to see
That there is no bliss there.

But at dusk, in the thin rain,
We passed without stopping
A half-ruined station,
On the gray wall we saw
Written in big white letters:
LET ME DIE!

Four waitresses (one a lovely eagle)
Serve under the aegis of strong thugs.
The girls the soul, the thugs the body.

And one of them is a lovely eagle. On her narrow waist
A wide belt with a silver buckle.
The buckle is the answer.
No, the buckle is the riddle,
The belt is the answer.

Far away in a closed valley
The evening wind blows
From one place to another place.

On the broad sidewalk across from the university gate
An old woman sits in a wheelchair.
On doctor's orders she sits here
So that the stream of young people will inundate her
Every single day, like the healing waters of a spa.

You live in your permanent home
Across from my temporary home.
Only the street separates us.
At night its white lines
As the white of an eye.

When you're not at home, the lights are on in your window,
When you're there, everything is dark.
Your hair is laughter and weeping all at once,
In your soul a tiny hole for stringing,
You wear your soul like a necklace.

Farewell, I must return to my land
For I begin to know the names of trees
And flowers of your land. Hence I must return.
I gave you flowers smuggled out of Eden
Into a world of thorns and the sweat of your brow,
You gave me scented powders
For bubbles in a soothing bath.

Farewell.
You too a knife
That didn't mean to be a knife.

# THE LAUNDRY CELLAR

The laundry cellar in the big house. I love to
Be there, in the lower heaven, while outside,
In the high windows, the world in its noisy evil.

The laundry cellar. The meeting place of the
Gray-haired, angry man and the girl, naked
Under her last sheet on her body,
The rest of her clothes, underwear and upperwear,
Heaven and hell together
Spinning in dizzy excitement
In the drums of the machine, like games of chance
For the redistribution of destinies and bodies.

The laundry cellar. Among the sweet soap vapors
A great desire sweeps up in me
To change my life from beginning to end.
I embrace the fragrant, warm basket
And go up in the drunk elevator,
Like a person dreaming a dream within a dream
Who has to wake up
Once and once more
To return to This World.

Four waitresses talking in the tongue
Of the Isle of Malta. In their mouths, resurrection
Of mortal enemies, Crusaders and Moslems,
Their sweet chatter mixes them, like history,
Words make peace.

One wears her hair tight on her scalp
Like a helmet. She mixes drinks
Ringing spoon and goblet. She knows
The soul is made of glass.

Wineglasses on a shelf,
Upside down, quiet.

And gleaming lies for a fast screw.

In front of the big window, they're digging a pit in the street,
The shame of the earth is revealed in the open,
Like a drunkard, with torn clothes, dirty.
A surveyor puts his binoculars
On her thin legs and measures straight lines
Through everything, as through an empty desert.

And a young woman at a nearby table
Said to another woman: "I got a small part
In a new play: to enter the room,
Pass through it and exit the other side."
She said this and got up to go.

Stay here, stay here near me,
Stay at least until one prophecy is fulfilled.
But she left, and I stayed. Half the cake
On my plate and half inside me.
The spoon fell on the floor.

Sometimes a man bends to pick up something
That fell out of his hand, and when he gets up,
The world has changed.

Here soft hills touch the sea,
As eternity touching another eternity.
And the cows grazing on them
Ignore us, like angels.
Even the smell of the ripe melon in the cellar
Is a prophecy of calm.

Dark doesn't fight light,
But transfers us further on
To another light and the only pain
Is the pain of not remaining.

In my own land called holy
They won't let eternity be eternity:
They divided it into small religions
And parceled into parcels of gods
And broke it down into shards of history,
Sharp and mortally wounding.
And turned its calm distances
Into closeness trembling in the pain of the present.

On Bolinas Beach, at the foot of the wooden stairs,
I saw bare-assed girls
Sprawling in the sand face down,
Intoxicated with the kingdom of all the worlds
And their souls inside them like doors
Open and close,
Open and close,
In the rhythm of the breakers.

The quiet man showed me around campus,
His dead wife accompanied us, pleasant as heaven.
Girls lying on the lawn, God lying in heaven.

In this pretty place, between the fragrant flowerbeds,
The luxurious library building is meaningless.
Libraries are like orphanages,
The books stand there still, in straight lines,
The parents of the words died long ago.
And all that happened, as if it never happened.
History is the transmission of great weariness
To new, fresh people, like the girls
Sunbathing here almost naked in the grass,
Waiting for sunset
To make them even more beautiful.

# Even a Fist Once
# Was an Open Palm
# and Fingers

❋❋❋❋ ❦❦❦❦

1989

## Tel Gath

I brought my children to the mound
Where once I fought battles,
So they would understand the things I did do
And forgive me for the things I didn't do.

The distance between my striding legs and my head
Grows bigger and I grow smaller.
Those days grow away from me,
These times grow away from me too,
And I'm in the middle, without them, on this mound
With my children.

A light afternoon wind blows
But only a few people move in the blowing wind,
Bend down a little with the grass and the flowers.
Dandelions cover the mound.
You could say, as dandelions in multitude.

I brought my children to the mound
And we sat there, "on its back and its side"
As in the poem by Shmuel Ha-Nagid in Spain,
Like me, a man of hills and a man of wars,
Who sang a lullaby to his soldiers before the battle.

Yet I did not talk to my heart, as he did,
But to my children. To the mound, we were the resurrection,
Fleeting like this springtime, eternal like it too.

# Ruhama

In this wadi, we camped in the days of the war.
Many years have passed since, many victories,
Many defeats. Many consolations I gathered in my life
And wasted, much sorrow have I collected and spilled out in vain,
Many things I said, like the waves of the sea
In Ashkelon, to the west, always saying the same things.
But as long as I live, my soul remembers
And my body ripens slowly in the flame of its own annals.

The evening sky bends down like the sound of a trumpet
Above us, and the lips move like lips in a prayer
Before there was any God in the world.

Here we lay by day, and at night we went to battle.
The smell of the sand as it was, and the smell of eucalyptus leaves
As it was, and the smell of the wind as it was.

And I do now what every memory dog does:
I howl quietly
And piss a turf of remembrance around me,
No one may enter it.

# Huleikat—the Third Poem about Dicky

In these hills, even the towers of oil wells
Are a mere memory. Here Dicky fell,
Four years older than me, like a father to me
In times of trouble and distress. Now I am older than him
By forty years and I remember him
Like a young son, and I am his father, old and grieving.

And you, who remember only faces,
Do not forget the hands stretched out,
The feet running lightly,
The words.

Remember: even the departure to terrible battles
Passes by gardens and windows
And children playing, a dog barking.

Remind the fallen fruit
Of its leaves and branches,
Remind the sharp thorns
How soft and green they were in springtime,
And do not forget,
Even a fist
Was once an open palm and fingers.


## The Shore of Ashkelon

Here, at the shore of Ashkelon, we reached the end of memory,
Like rivers reaching the sea.
The near past sinks into the far past,
And from the depths, the far overflows the near.
Peace to him that is far off and to him that is near.

Here, among broken statues and pillars,
I ask how did Samson bring down the temple
Standing eyeless, saying: "Let me die with the Philistines."

Did he embrace the pillars as in a last love
Or did he push them away with his arms,
To be alone in his death.


## What Did I Learn in the Wars

What did I learn in the wars:
To march in time to swinging arms and legs
Like pumps pumping an empty well.

To march in a row and be alone in the middle,

To dig into pillows, featherbeds, the body of a beloved woman,
And to yell "Mama," when she cannot hear,
And to yell "God," when I don't believe in Him,
And even if I did believe in Him
I wouldn't have told Him about the war
As you don't tell a child about grown-ups' horrors.

What else did I learn. I learned to reserve a path for retreat.
In foreign lands I rent a room in a hotel
Near the airport or railroad station.
And even in wedding halls
Always to watch the little door
With the "Exit" sign in red letters.

A battle too begins
Like rhythmical drums for dancing and ends
With a "retreat at dawn." Forbidden love
And battle, the two of them sometimes end like this.

But above all I learned the wisdom of camouflage,
Not to stand out, not to be recognized,
Not to be apart from what's around me,
Even not from my beloved.
Let them think I am a bush or a lamb,
A tree, a shadow of a tree,
A doubt, a shadow of a doubt,
A living hedge, a dead stone,
A house, a corner of a house.

If I were a prophet I would have dimmed the glow of the vision
And darkened my faith with black paper
And covered the magic with nets.

And when my time comes, I shall don the camouflage garb of my end:
The white of clouds and a lot of sky blue
And stars that have no end.

### Anniversary of Love

Anniversary of love. A hymn from the forties.
Letters like banners waving in the wind
Or folded in a cupboard. Bound up in our bundles.

"I live among orange groves,
Ramatayim or Giv'at Haim,
I live near the water tower.
I draw from it great strength and great love,
You will understand in years to come."

The stalk releases its smell when you break it,
Leaves release their smell when you rub them
Thinly between your fingers. So will our love be,
You will understand in years to come.

You will cross great distances,
But you never were in the distance between my eyes
And you never will be. You will understand.
You will be in places with no orange groves,
You will forget this love
As you forgot the child's voice
You once had. You will understand in years to come.

### But, We

Far away, the war started. But we
Were at home. The future was close by,
It started just outside the window.

The future was yellow, the color of acacias,
And purple like bougainvillea, and its voices were
The voices of the two of us.

We loved in the orchard on the sand,
The orchard gave us its strength and we gave it ours.
Beyond the row of cypresses a train passed,
But we only heard it, didn't see.
And all the words we spoke between us
Began with "but we."

And when we parted, when the war was over
These words too parted: the word "but"
Remained there, the word "we" moved somewhere else.


## Sixty Kilograms of Pure Love

Sixty kilograms of pure love, net femininity
Built for splendor that built itself—
With no architects' blueprints, no beginning, no end.
Passionate, pure autogenetics:
A love cell begets a love cell.

What does the environment do to you,
What do changes do to you?
They make you beautiful on the outside, like a sunset,
And tickle you on the inside. You laugh,
I love you.


## In the Migration of Peoples

And though we lived in the same corridor
In the same house, we met only as two strangers
Meeting in the migration of peoples in ancient times,
By chance.

And though you are younger than me by many years,
We are both of the same archaeological stratum in the future.

You take words from the same place as me,
But your words are different from mine.

The light in your hair, like the light
Caught in an old photo.

Housekeys used to be big and heavy and separate
And very quiet. Now bundles of keys
Small and flat, rattle and tinkle,
Know a lot.

Now they write names on shirts,
Once they were carved on stone.

I will be different
Like a tree made
Into useful furniture.

And you will remain there beautiful
Like rare glass vessels in a museum,
Never again to be filled
With oil and milk, wine and mead.


## Two Disappeared in the House

Two disappeared in the house.
The stone of the steps soothes the feet of those who ascend
As the stone that soothes the feet of those who descend,
As the stone that soothes the dead in their graves.
And the more the steps ascend
The less they are used,
The highest ones are like new—
For souls that leave no traces.
Like people living in high regions:
When they speak, their voices rise more melodious,
Up to the singing of the angels.

Two disappeared in the house.
They turn on a light. They turn it off.
The staircase goes out through the roof into the space of night
Like an unfinished building.


## In the History of Our Love

In the history of our love, always one is
A nomadic tribe, the other a nation on its own soil.
When we changed places, it was all over.

Time will pass us by, as landscapes
Move behind actors standing in their places
When they make a movie. Even the words
Will pass by our lips, even the tears
Will pass by our eyes. Time will pass
Every one in his place.

And in the geography of the rest of our lives,
Who will be an island and who a peninsula
Will become clear to each of us in the rest of our lives
In nights of love with others.


## In-Between

Where will we be when these flowers turn into fruit
In the narrow in-between, when the flower is no longer a flower
And the fruit is not yet fruit. And what a wonderful in-between did we
     make
For each other, between body and body. In-between eyes, between waking
     and sleep.
In-between twilight, not day, not night.

How your springtime dress became a summer banner,
And there it's waving in the first autumn wind.


416     *Yehuda Amichai*

How my voice was my voice no more
But, almost, like prophecy.

What a wonderful in-between we were, like soil
In the cracks of a wall, small, stubborn earth
For the bold moss, the thorny caper bush
Whose bitter fruit
Sweetened what we ate together.

These are the last days of books.
Then, the last days of words.
You will understand in years to come.

## I Know a Man

I know a man
Who took pictures of the landscape he saw
From the window of the room where he loved
And not of the face of the one he loved.

# FROM JERUSALEM TO THE SEA AND BACK

### From Enclosed Jerusalem

I went from enclosed Jerusalem toward the open sea
As to the opening of a will. I went
On the old road. A bit before Ramla,
On the side of the road, still stand
Tall, strange hangars,
Half-ruined, from the World War:
There they checked engines of airplanes,
Their noise silenced the whole world.
Pure flying was hoarded then
For all my life.

### The Soul

I travel. Travels are the soul
Of this world. Travels remain forever.
It's so simple: a green mountain slope growing trees and grass,
On the other side a dry mountain slope, charred by the hot wind,
I travel between them. Simple logic of the sunny side
And the rainy side. Blessing and curse, justice and injustice,
I travel between them. Wind of the sky and wind of the earth,
Wind against me and wind with me. Hot love and cold love
Like the migration of birds. Travel, my car.

## Not Far from Death

In Latrun,* not far from the death on the hill
And the silence in the buildings, stands a woman
On the side of the road. Next to her, a shiny new car,
Motor gaping in amazement, waiting
To be towed to a safe place.
The woman is beautiful. Her face, confidence and rage.
Her dress a love banner. A very passionate woman,
Inside her stands her dead father
Like a quiet soul. I knew him alive,
I greeted him when I passed by.


## An Old Bus Stop

I passed an old bus stop where I stood
Many years ago, waiting for a vehicle to take me
Someplace else.

There I stood, consoled before loss
And healed before pain, resurrected
Before death and full of love before separation.

There I stood. The groggy fragrance
Of orange groves in blossom anesthetized me
For all the years to come, to this very day.

The stop is still there. God is still
Called "Place," and I, sometimes,
Call Him "Time."


*A Trappist monastery and the site of a fierce battle in the Israeli War of Independence.

## Sunflower Fields

Fields of sunflowers ripe and withering,
Brown and wise, need the sun no more but sweet
Shadow, internalized death, the inside of a drawer,
A sack deep as the sky, their World-to-Come,
Dark of a house, the inside of a man.

## I at the Sea

I at the sea. Sailboats of many colors move
Over the water. Next to them, I am a clumsy oil tanker
With a small white poopdeck,
My body is heavy and my head small, thinking
Or not thinking. Did think.

In the sand I saw a girl learning to dress
Or undress in public under a huge towel:
What a wonderful dance of her body. What a hidden serpent movement,
What a struggle between dressing and undressing,
Between Jacob and his angel, between lover and beloved.

The towel drops from her body as from a statue unveiled.
The girl won. She laughs. She waits.
And perhaps they wait for her in a tearful place.
She is more beautiful than me, and younger.
I am more prophet than her.

## And I Return

And I return to Jerusalem. I sit on my seat
But my soul stands inside me like a congregation praying:
Holy, Holy, Holy. Travel, my car.
On a small hill beside the road tanks were standing,

No more. Now carob trees at dusk,
A male carob and a female carob from another world that is pure love.
The tremor of their leaves in the wind is like the tremor of precision
    instruments
Measuring the unmeasurable.
And the shadows that will merge and will be called night,
And we who will be called by our full names
By which we are called only in death.

The night of never-again will come again.
I return to my home in Jerusalem and our names will be lost
Among these hills like shouts from the mouths of searchers.

## FOUR RESURRECTIONS IN THE VALLEY OF THE GHOSTS

### First Resurrection

A woman who looks like my mother sees a man who looks like me,
They pass each other without turning around.

Mistakes are marvelous and simple as life and death,
As the arithmetic book of a small child.

In the shelter for wayward girls, girls singing on the balcony
Hang their clothes out to dry, banners of love.

In the fiber institute they make ropes of fiber
To bind souls in the bundle of life.

An afternoon wind blows, as if asking:
What did you do, what did you talk about.

In old stone houses young women do in the day
What the mothers of their mothers dreamed of doing at night.

The Armenian church is empty and closed
Like an abandoned wife whose husband went far off and disappeared.

Wayward girls sing, "God will bring the dead to life
In His great mercy" and fold their dried clothes.
"Blessed forever be His name."

### Second Resurrection

In the public park, pots that once held plants—
Now empty and crumpled like discarded wombs.

Seesaws and slides, like instruments of torture,
Or like wings of a big bird or a falling angel.

And the ancient ceremony begins,
A father tells his little son:

"So I'm going,
And you stay here alone."

So are summer and winter in their due time, so are
Generations in their changes, so those who remain, those who go.


### Third Resurrection

With the pleading voice of a beggar
I praise the world.

With a voice crying for help from the depths,
I laud.

A young woman curses her mother
Who left her fat thighs.

I bless her,
And her too.

The sadness of parted lovers is empty here, hollow as a drum.

People wrote on the gate of their home:
"Strangers No Entrance"
But they themselves are strangers.

At the wall of the Christian cemetery
A violated telephone booth,
The torn wires hanging, like veins
And arteries: waiting for their time.

## Fourth Resurrection

I saw the seats of a torn-down movie house
Lying in an empty lot,
Taken out of their dark home
And abandoned to the cruel sun,
Broken seats with fragments of numbered rows:
24, 26, 28, 30 with 7, 9, 11, 13.

And I asked myself: Where are the feats and where are the words
That were on the screen. *Who in fire and who in water,*
And where are those who sat in these seats,
Where is their lament and where is their laughter,
Where are their roads and where are their oaths,
And what are the sights and the images they see,
And what are the words they hear now.
Are they still sitting in numbered rows
Or standing in long lines,
And how will they arise to life and where.

# ❧ I AM A POOR PROPHET ❧

I am a poor prophet. Like a poor boy with only
Two colors: I paint my life in war
And in love, in clamor and in silence.

The great prophets threw out half their prophecies
Like the half-smoked cigarette butts of a nervous smoker.
I pick them up and roll myself some poor prophecies.

In full water towers the water is silent,
In empty pipes, the no-water gurgles and snores.

Words soak up "blood, sweat, and tears"
And are thrown out in the ashcan. Disposable words,
Like Kleenex. Disposable people,
This is their eternity.

Words should have been empty
And narrow and tough, like a watershed.
Despair and hope, joy and sorrow, calm and rage
Should have floated in the two sides,
In a new cycle.

I am a poor prophet. I live inside the hope of others
As inside a beam of light not meant for me.
I cast a shadow in my own image.
My body blocks a famous and beautiful view,
I come between the seer and the sight.

I am a prophet with no profit who comes back home at lunchtime
To eat and rest and at night to sleep.
I have an annual vacation, a sabbatical,
Soul Security and a retirement pension.

I started my life so low.
When I climb high with my intoxicated soul,

When I reach the peak of my visions,
I find myself with everyday people
Who have children and work, family cares,
Household chores. These are my visions.
I am a poor prophet.

## SUMMER EVENING AT THE
## WINDOW WITH PSALMS

Careful examination of the past.
*Why is my soul disquieted within me* like the souls
In the nineteenth century before the great wars,
Like curtains that want to free themselves
From the open window and fly away.

We console ourselves with short breaths
As after running. We heal ourselves
Always. We want to reach death
Hale and healthy, like a murderer
Condemned to death, wounded when he was caught,
Whom the judges want to recover before the gallows.

I think: how many *still waters*
Can give one still night,
And how many *green pastures*, wide as the desert,
Will give one hour of peace,
And how many *valleys of the shadow of death* do we need
To cast a shadow full of compassion in the cruel sun.

I look through the window: one hundred and fifty
Psalms pass through the twilight,
One hundred and fifty Psalms, big and small,
What a great, splendid, passing fleet!

I say: the window is God
And the door is His prophet.

## ➤ SUMMER REST ➤
## AND WORDS

The sprinklers calm summer's wrath.
The sound of the sprinkler twirling
And the swish of the water on leaves and grass
Are enough for me. My wrath
Spent and calm and my melancholy full and quiet.
The newspaper drops from my hand and turns back into
Passing times and paper wings.
I shut my eyes,
And return to the words of the rabbi in my childhood
On the bimah of the synagogue: "And give eternal salvation
To those who go off to their world." He changed
The words of the prayer a little, he did not
Sing and did not trill and did not sob
And did not flatter his God like a cantor
But said his words with quiet confidence, demanded of God
In a calm voice that accompanied me all my life.

What did he mean by these words,
Is there salvation only for those who go to their rest?
And what about our world and what about mine?
Is rest salvation or is there any other?
And why did he add eternity to salvation?
Words accompany me. Words accompany my life
Like a melody. Words accompany my life
As at the bottom of a movie screen, subtitles
Translating their language into mine.

I remember, in my youth the translation sometimes
Lagged behind the words, or came before them,
The face on the screen was sad, even crying,
And words below were joyful, or things lit up
And laughed and the words spelled great sadness.
Words accompany my life.

But the words I say myself
Are now like stones I fling
Into a well in the field, to test
If it is full or empty,
And its depth.

## AUTUMN IS NEAR AND MEMORY OF MY PARENTS

Autumn is near. The last fruit ripens.
People walk on roads they never walked on.
The old house begins to forgive its tenants.
Trees darken with age and people whiten.
Rain will come. The smell of rust will be fresh
And pleasant like the smell of blossoming in the spring.

In the northern countries they say most leaves
Are still on the trees, and here we say
Most words are still on the people,
Our foliage loses other things.

Autumn is near. Time to remember my parents.
I remember them like the simple
Toys of my childhood
Revolving in little circles,
Humming quietly, raising a leg,
Lifting an arm, turning a head
From side to side, rhythmically, slowly,
A spring in their belly and the key in their back.

Suddenly, freezing, they remain
Forever in their last gesture.

That is how I remember my parents.
And how they were.

## ➤ LITTLE RUTH ❦

Sometimes I remember you, little Ruth,
We were separated in our distant childhood and they burned you in the
　　camps.
If you were alive now, you would be a woman of sixty-five,
A woman on the verge of old age. At twenty you were burned
And I don't know what happened to you in your short life
Since we separated. What did you achieve, what insignia
Did they put on your shoulders, your sleeves, your
Brave soul, what shining stars
Did they pin on you, what decorations for valor, what
Medals for love hung around your neck,
What peace upon you, *peace unto you.*
And what happened to the unused years of your life?
Are they still packed away in pretty bundles,
Were they added to my life? Did you turn me
Into your bank of love like the banks in Switzerland
Where assets are preserved even after their owners are dead?
Will I leave all this to my children
Whom you never saw?

You gave your life to me, like a wine dealer
Who remains sober himself.
You sober in death, lucid in the dark
For me, drunk on life, wallowing in my forgetfulness.
Now and then, I remember you in times
Unbelievable. And in places not made for memory
But for the transient, the passing that does not remain.
As in an airport, when the arriving travelers
Stand tired at the revolving conveyor belt
That brings their suitcases and packages,
And they identify theirs with cries of joy
As at a resurrection and go out into their lives;
And there is one suitcase that returns and disappears again
And returns again, ever so slowly, in the empty hall,

*A Life of Poetry*　431

Again and again it passes.
This is how your quiet figure passes by me,
This is how I remember you until
The conveyor belt stands still. *And they stood still. Amen.*

# ❧ SHEEPSKIN COAT ❧

My good friend gave me a sheepskin coat
On a cold winter day in a distant land.
The coat turned me into an inside-out sheep,
The woolly fur inside and the skin outside,
I am an internalized sheep maaing inside.
I don't know if the coat will keep off rain and snow
Or will absorb them and make me heavy,
But it will protect my internal world.
My internal world perhaps is no more
Than a collection of rags and junk
The crazy collector gathered to soothe himself.
And maybe I do not live inside my life,
Like a streetlamp, its light living
In a dark room while it stands outside.

The coat is brown on the outside and white inside.
My eyes are earth-colored, my shirt the color of a green field,
But fields do not give me bread, stores do.
And the twilight wind does not move stalks in the field
But buyers in shining halls
And people no longer for human use
But only for vain ornament—like horses,
Or like candles, once used for light
And now only for a passing holiday or a fleeting memory.
Everything changes. Everything changes,
Sleep shivers with cold and chaos,
Memories explode and sink like ashes,
Continuity bursts like a thin paper bag,
Every passing car tears off of me
A layer of life, dreams are hard as ice
And cold as ice and melt like ice and are forgotten like water.
Times change places and landscapes move to another place
But I remain like a telephone pole
Without wires above,

I am faithful as a water pipe,
Even when the water streams in other channels.

My friend gave me a sheepskin coat made
In a distant place in the Andes Mountains:
Gave me warmth from overseas, indulgence from afar.
I did not see the sheep alive or their shepherds,
I did not see the meadow or the hands
That stroked this sheep or the hands
That slaughtered it and skinned it
Or the mouths that ate its meat
And sang songs of high mountains after they ate their fill.

The sheepskin coat is alien among the sheep of our land
Who slide down the Hermon and graze in the mountains of Ephraim.
But it will get used to it as people do,
Like the eucalyptus trees who brought their fragrance from afar,
Without forgetting, without getting tough,
Like the soft Bible in a hard binding
I still want to kiss with my lips
When it falls from the table to the floor.

# MAN WITH KNAPSACK

Man with knapsack in the marketplace, Brother,
Like you, I am a donkey man, a camel man,
An angel man, I am like you.
Our arms are free like wings.
Compared to us, all who carry full baskets
Are slaves of slaves bound and pulled down.

We exchange coins for fresh vegetables,
And for the forgetting of our lives we buy
Fruit and their memories, memory of field and garden,
Memory of the smell of earth and the buzzing of bees on a hot day.

We saw a woman in a light summer dress
Before a great and heavy love
Which will determine her life. She doesn't know yet
But we do. On our back
We carry fruit from the tree of knowledge.

Man with knapsack, where do you live?
I am like you, we live in the distances
Between reward and punishment.
And how do you live? And how do you sleep at night,
What do you dream of? People you love,
Do they still live in the same places?

Our knapsacks like folded parachutes
On our backs, at night they open wide
So we can jump, hovering
Into the fragrance of remembering and forgetting.

You are the *rose of Sharon, the lily of the valleys*
And I an aging male animal full of memories
About the Sharon and the valleys and lots of lilies.

*I gave my back to the smiters,* my tears
I turned into perfume, my sweat into spice
And my sighs into a soothing melody,
The cycle of my blood wells up in me
Like the cycle of prayers on holidays.

You knead me as your hands please,
Strong hands *like the hands of Esau from the field*
And sweet *like the voice of Jacob.*
The traces of clothes on my skin are erased
Like the traces of tefillin from my childhood, like traces
Of hard straps from my wars,
Like traces of this world
That will be erased in the world to come.

You turned my body into my soul,
The soles of my feet into a face
(And they sing hallelujah).
The triple brain between my legs is light and thoughtless,
The ass is the messiah full of salvation,
An all-forgetting messiah.

My mouth sucks on the cracks of closed windows
And on keyholes of locked doors,
My mouth sucks and I fill up like a baby,
Like a sated bedbug landed on his back.
Silly baby sucking everywhere,
"Silly baby! Suck, don't bite,
You're hurting, you're spoiling it all."

436    *Yehuda Amichai*

You left and I was left lying
Like chairs in a restaurant at night overturned
On a table, legs spread and hands up
As in a prayer, a vain prayer.

With no yesterday no tomorrow
No beginning and no end
Like God
Without God.

## ✦ THE GREATEST DESIRE OF ALL ✦

Instead of singing hallelujah, a curtain waves in an open window.
Instead of saying amen, a door closes, a shutter is shut.
Instead of the vision of the end of days
The voice of banners flapping in an empty street after a holiday.

Reflections take over the house,
Float in the mirror, in the goblet.

I saw slivers of glass gleaming in the sun
In the Judean Desert, celebrating a wedding
With no groom no bride, pure celebration.

I saw a big and beautiful parade passing in the street,
I saw policemen standing between the spectators and the procession,
Their faces to the viewers,
Their backs to all that passed with trumpets and joy and banners.
Perhaps to live like this.

But the greatest desire of all is to be
In the dream of another,
To feel a slight pull, like reins,
To feel a heavy pull, like chains.

## DEIR AYUB, A HEAP OF
## WATERMELONS AND THE
## REST OF MY LIFE

Deir Ayub, a heap of watermelons and the rest of my life.
An attack of sweetness in the room. I hear
The sound of passing cars outside and the sound of an airplane in the sky
Like a dialogue at a nearby table and suddenly
An erection. The words from both sides of the equation
Part from one another. Only the equal sign remains
Like a buckle, for the release from a vow, an oath,
For the release of a buckle in love. Attack of sweetness in the room.

Deir Ayub at the entrance to the valley,
Heap of watermelons next to the wall
And the rest of my life here. I hear the children of my childhood
Sing songs for the memory of the dead, "*Therefore*
*My heart is glad and my glory rejoiceth but my flesh*
*Shall rest in hope,*" and suddenly—erection.
Like the erection when you wake from a dream
Which remains, even when the dream is forgotten.

CHANGES, MISTAKES, LOVES

In the summer, in a big park among the trees, I saw
A young man and a young woman photographing one another
On the lawn sloping down. Then they change places
And whoever comes in his place and in her place, will be
Like the difference between a cypress and a pine.

Oh changes, oh mistakes,
Most loves are a mistake like the mistake of Columbus
Who came to America and thought he had reached India
And called the continent India,
So lovers say love,
The land of my love, my love.

Oh dark snooker game,
Billiard balls clacking, falling into depths,
And the loneliness of one who remains alone at the table.

Oh tennis games in black garb
And nets eternally dividing.

In a very distant land, I once heard a girl
Playing on a violin *"Eli, eli,
She-lo yigamer le-olam"* so sweetly.*

On a violin, with no words, far from the death
Of Hannah Senesh and far from the white shore.
The same song, perhaps a love song to God,
Perhaps to man, perhaps to the sea, perhaps
Caesarea, perhaps Hungary,
Perhaps death, perhaps life.

*"My God, my God, let it never end." From a Hebrew song by Hannah Senesh, a native of Hungary and member of Kibbutz Sdot Yam (Caesarea), who parachuted into occupied Hungary during World War II and was caught and executed by the Nazis.

# THE FIRST RAIN ON A BURNED CAR

Life close to death
At the body of a car on the roadside.

You hear the drops of rain on rusty tin
Before you feel them on the skin of your face.

Rain came, salvation after death.
Rust more eternal than blood, more beautiful than the color of flames.

Shock absorbers calmer than the dead
Who will not calm down for a long time.

Wind that is time alternates
With wind that is place, and God
Remains on earth like a man who thinks
He forgot something and stays
Until he remembers.

And at night you can hear,
Like a wonderful melody, man and machine
On their slow road from a red fire
To black peace and from there to history
And from there to archaeology and from there
To the beautiful strata of geology,
This too is eternity and great happiness.

Like human sacrifice that turned into animal
Sacrifice and then into prayer with a loud voice,
And then into prayer in the heart
And then without prayer.

# RAMATAYIM

People sit on the porch
Like ancient heroes at their tent door
Recovering from imaginary wounds.

Their voices hanging on the banister
Like clothes drying, pants and undershirts,
Shirts and underpants, thigh's moaning and knee's crying,
Song of legs and womb, screams of neck and armpit,
The cut off laughter of a breast.

From the wall, faucets stand out like prophets,
Some running, some off.

Bread and circuses go on all summer,
Statistics and eternal pain,
Summer accounts and planning for the end,
The end of the day and the end of all days.
On the wall a painting of the sunset
In a snowy northern land, the sun itself
Sets beyond the last orange grove.
(A woman's scent like the scent of citrus blossoms.)

The watch souls begin to bark,
The sweet cake wounded to death,
Sugar fell in the war.

Water from last night in the puddles,
Seeds from last season in the earth,
The earth from thousands of years ago.

All the things that happened before I was born,
At a time when they called the newborn
By the name of what happened when he was born
And the hills by the name of a beautiful god
And the springs by the name of love or death.

Reeds grow at the water
But also at the memory of water.
In the sky God's hammocks.
And among the palms and eucalyptus trees—
What's left for a man
But to surrender himself in happiness,
To donate his blood and his kidneys,
To donate his heart and his soul to others,
To belong to another, to be another.

In the old graveyard, buried together,
One dead of cholera and a baby that died at birth,
And Eve, daughter of Erich Falk, who died
At eighteen years of age, far from her father's home.

And all the things that happened before I was born
Meet the things that will happen after my death
And enclose me all around
And leave me behind
Far away, forgotten and calm.

And what was sown by mistake of a wind was absorbed in the earth,
And what was flown by the caprice of a bee lives on,
And what was spread unwittingly by a passing shoe
Goes on growing by its laws and its cycles,

And what laughed by mistake goes on laughing,
And what cried weeps in the rain,
And what died by error
Goes on resting in death.

"I never was in Hadera" is like
A verdict killing by sorrow and establishing a fact, like death.
"I just passed through and didn't stay."

The Street of the Heroes I understand,
I understand heroes and their death.
The water tower I understand,
But I never stayed in Hadera.

The roads of my life I thought were roads
Were only light bridges
Above places where I never was.

In the old house the tiles still perform
The tapping of a dance that was.
Hosts forgot whom they invited
Guests didn't know they were invited
And didn't come and those who could have met didn't meet.

People had hopes like eucalyptuses,
They were brought from far away and remained.
And in the abandoned orchard, citrus trees beg
For a fence around them as a soul
Begs for a body again. The pumping shed is ruined,
An old engine rusting outside like an old man at the end of his days
Sitting in the door of his house, full of years,
At his side the remnants of a spring, throbbing weakly
In the scum of a shallow swamp, as a memory.

What determined my life and what didn't.
Oh summer 1942, oh Hadera
Where I only passed by and didn't stay.
Had I stayed my life would be different.

People scratched their names
On walls of the cave and went off or died,
Thus their souls were created, names and souls.

Oh, my dead, my landscapes, my skies,
I am so heavy and aimless
Like weights without a scale.

And once I was a scale without weights,
Rising and falling easily, like a swing.

The voice of a turtledove laments even at its wedding
And the bees in their white hives
Make real honey here in the dry hills
Far from the blossom of the lush Sharon.

I saw children roaming and heard their merriment
Passing from one cave to another.

Oh, holy despair of parents,
Oh, sweet disappointment of teachers,
Oh, their smell and oh, their spirit.

Words come to me now like flies
And like wasps, they are drawn to the wet in me
And the dry in me, to the sweet and to the bitter in me,
To the full and to the empty,
To the living and the dead and the rotting in me,
To the dark in me and to the light. Words forever.

"What kind of a person are you," I heard them say to me.
I'm a person with a complex plumbing of the soul,
Sophisticated instruments of feeling and a system
Of controlled memory at the end of the twentieth century,
But with an old body from ancient times
And with a God even older than my body.

I'm a person for the surface of the earth.
Low places, caves and wells
Frighten me. Mountain peaks
And tall buildings scare me.

I'm not like an inserted fork,
Not a cutting knife, not a stuck spoon.
I'm not flat and sly
Like a spatula creeping up from below.
At most I am a heavy and clumsy pestle
Mashing good and bad together
For a little taste
And a little fragrance.

Arrows do not direct me. I conduct
My business carefully and quietly
Like a long will that began to be written
The moment I was born.

Now I stand at the side of the street
Weary, leaning on a parking meter.
I can stand here for nothing, free.

I'm not a car, I'm a person,
A man-god, a god-man
Whose days are numbered. Hallelujah.

Open window. On the television screen colors
Caper and tremble, like life flickering out,
Shoes strewn over the floor,
Clothes on the chair and no person.
On a stretched line underwear drying
From the flood of forty days and forty nights.
Open closet like a face you remember,
On the table flowers with long stalks
Like the roads of life a man snipped
And put in a vase.

Here too the question arises, where did they go,
Where does all this lead.

In the restaurant on the sidewalk opposite, a woman sits
At a table, her gaze raised above her plate,
She connects with a distant satellite in space.
Prepares to take off.

## LIKE THE STREAMS IN THE NEGEV

I sit in a café in the afternoon hours.
My sons are grown, my daughter is dancing somewhere else.
I have no baby carriage, no newspaper, no God.

I saw a woman whose father was with me in the battles of the Negev,
I saw his eyes gaping in a time of trouble
And dread of death. Now they are in the face of his daughter,
Quiet, beautiful eyes. The rest of her body—
From other places. Her hair grew in a time of peace,
A different genetics, generations and times I didn't know.

I have many times, like many watches
On the walls of a clock shop, each one shows a different time.
My memories are scattered over the earth
Like the ashes of a person who willed before his death
To burn his body
And scatter his ashes over seven seas.

I sit. Voices talking around me
Like fine ironwork on a banister,
Beyond it I hear the street. The table before me
Is built for easy access like a bay,
Like a pier in a port, like God's hand, like bride and groom.

Sometimes tears of happiness well up in me
As an empty street suddenly fills up with cars
When the light changes at a distant intersection,
Or as the streams in the Negev
Suddenly fill up with torrents of water from a distant rain.
Afterward, again silence, empty
*Like the streams in the Negev, like the streams in the Negev.*

An empty can on a rock
Lit by the last rays of the sun.
A child throws stones at it,
The can tumbles, the stone falls,
The sun goes down. Between things that go down
And fall I seem to rise,
A new Isaac Newton canceling the laws of nature.
My penis like a pinecone
Closed on many cells of seed.

I hear the children playing. Wild grapes too
Are descendants unto the third generation.
Voices too are sons and great-grandsons
Of voices lost forever in their joy.

In these mountains hope belongs to the place
Like cisterns. Even those empty
Still belong to the place like hope.

I open my mouth and sing into the world.
I have a mouth, the world has no mouth.
It must use mine if it wants
To sing into me. I and the world are equivalent.
I am more.

# ✦ SURPLUS OF FLOWERS ✦
## IN THE WORLD

Surplus of flowers in the world
Like the surplus of the coffee crop in Brazil
Thrown into the sea. Surplus of flowers
Adorns tables in empty rooms and tombstones.

The movement of trade in the world calms me
Like the migration of birds. And a torn newspaper with a date
Fluttering on the floor makes me feel light.

Fog enfolds the end of one year
And the beginning of the next. I am excused from knowing
What is in the future beyond the fog.

I am a useless watchman
Of the holy nothing. I am happy.
I am like an artilleryman bereft of
His target and his enemies and his God
And his shells and his cannon.
He aims at emptiness, he aims
His face and his face is beaming.

Sometimes I still hear the world
And all that's in it, like a little boy who puts a watch to his ear
And hears the ticktock without understanding.

In my childhood I had two old aunts
Who had a sofa and on the sofa
They tickled me with long knitting needles, and on the sofa
Were throw pillows embroidered with
A swan and an angel and roses.

They embroidered and embroidered the world on the pillows
And embroidered me too on the darkness of their death.
They loved me. I was their messiah.
And they said: A child should not be undressed
Or dressed by more than one person, because only
The dead are dressed by two or three after the cleansing.
And I was their messiah.

# ✥ YOM KIPPUR ✥

Yom Kippur without my father and without my mother
Is not Yom Kippur.

From the blessing of their hands on my head
Just the tremor has remained like the tremor of an engine
That didn't stop even after their death.

My mother died only five years ago,
She is still being processed
Between the offices above and the papers below.

My father who died long ago is already resurrected
In other places but not in my place.

Yom Kippur without my father and without my mother
Is not Yom Kippur.
Hence I eat to remember
And drink not to forget
And sort out the vows
And catalogue the oaths by time and size.

In the day we shouted *Forgive us,*
And in the evening we cried *Open to us.*
And I say forget our sins, forget us, leave us alone
At the closing of the gate when the day is done.
The last ray of the sun splintered
In the colored glass window of the synagogue.
The ray of the sun is not splintered,
We are splintered,
The word "splintered" is splintered.

A man's soul is like
A train schedule
A precise and detailed schedule
Of trains that will never run again.

Like high mountain climbers who set up a base in the valley at the foot
of the mountains and another camp and camp number two and camp
number three at various heights on the road to the peak, and in every
camp they leave food and provisions and equipment to make their last
climb easier and to collect on their way back everything that might help
them as they descend, so I leave my childhood and my youth and my
adult years in various camps with a flag on every camp. I know I shall
never return, but to get to the peak with no weight, light, light!

Traces that met in the sand were erased.
Their makers too were erased in the wind of their unbeing.

The little became a lot and what was a lot will become infinite
*As the sand on the seashore.* I found an envelope,
An address on its front and an address on its back.
But inside, empty and silent. The letter
Was read somewhere else, like a soul that left its body.

A happy tune that lingered at night in the big white house
Now is full of longing and full of sand
Like bathing suits hung on a line between two wooden poles.

Water birds scream when they see land
And people scream when they see calm.
Oh, my children, children of my head,
I made them with my whole body and my whole soul,
Now they are the children of my head,
Now I am alone on this shore
With sandweed, low and trembling.
This trembling is its language. This trembling is my language.
We have a common language.

A big anchor stuck in the yard. It will wait for eternity
For the ship it lost. Its longing adorns the world,
Its rust a banner for all that was lost and will not return.

And at the gate a heap of cannonballs
From centuries gone by. Balls that hit
And balls that missed. The collector did not distinguish.

From the roof, you see the western Galilee
Flourishing and green, the fat of the land. The road cuts
Through it deep, like the hems of a bathing suit tight on the flesh
Of thighs and derrieres. Desired land.

And in the house, a jumble of things.
A threshing sledge from an ancient vision,
A pitchfork from the prophecies and mills
Of dead people. Many tools to grind
And squeeze and crack and many tools to close and smooth,
Tools to build and tools to destroy,
As in the Book of Ecclesiastes. But above all
Handles whose tools were lost and only they remained.
What can we learn from this about the human soul
And all that was left. What can we learn
About the tools that were lost and the hands that held them.

At dusk the sun goes down in the sea
Like someone who heard about the death of a loved one.

A man returns from the sea holding his shoes
As if holding his soul in his hand.
A newspaper with a precise date flew away.
Two warships pass: one to the north, one to the south.
Day people change places with night people.
I see the changing of the guard in the beam of a flashlight.

On the mound over there, ancient graves open
At night. The opposite of flowers.

*Yehuda Amichai*

# ✦ I WANT TO CONFUSE ✦
## THE BIBLE

An airplane passes over the fig tree
That is over *the man under his fig tree.*
The pilot is me and the man under the fig tree is me.
I want to confuse the Bible.
I want so much to confuse the Bible.

I believe in trees, not as they once believed,
My belief is truncated and short-lived—
Till next spring, till next winter.
I believe in the coming of rain and in the coming of sun.
Order and justice are confused: good and evil
On the table before me like salt and pepper,
The shakers so alike. I want so much
To confuse the Bible. The world
Is filled with knowledge of good and evil, the world is filled
With learning: birds learn from the blowing wind,
Airplanes learn from the birds,
And people learn from all of them and forget.
The earth is not sad because the dead are buried in it.
As the dress of my beloved is not happy
That she lives in it.
The sons of man are clouds
And Ararat is a deep valley.
And I don't want to return home
Because all bad tidings come home
As in the Book of Job.

Abel killed Cain and Moses entered
The Promised Land and the Children of Israel stayed in the desert.
I travel in Ezekiel's divine chariot
And Ezekiel himself dances like Miriam
In the Valley of Dry Bones.
Sodom and Gomorrah are booming towns

And Lot's wife became a pillar of sugar and honey
And *David King of Israel is alive.*
I want so much
To confuse the Bible.

I don't know if I shall have a share in the World-to-Come,
But in the world of my children, I will have no share.

I am not a prophet and not the son of a prophet
But I am a father of prophets. My children
Light up the next century like spotlights.

Their games will be realized like prophecy
And their toys will come to life.
They are noise and silence and noise,
They are sea and land and air,
They are the skies and all their hosts.

Their longing for their future
And my longing for my childhood
Pass by one another without meeting
Like the fatal error of a tunnel engineer.

My daughter has little red shoes,
My two sons wear shoes my size,
But they don't have my father
And they don't have his God,
They have only me like a toy bear, big and hairy,
To stroke and play with,
So they will remember me and mention me to their children.
And they will remember that Ben Gurion was an airport
In the days when there still were airports
That remember the man and the rest of the deeds he did.

And I, sometimes, call the highway "King's Road,"
Though *there is no king in Israel*
*And everyone does what is right in his own eyes.*

The Jews are like photos in a display window,
All of them together, short and tall, alive and dead,
Brides and grooms, bar mitzvah boys and babies.
Some are restored from old yellowed photographs.
Sometimes people come and break the window
And burn the pictures. And then they start
Photographing and developing all over again
And displaying them again, sad and smiling.

Rembrandt painted them wearing Turkish
Turbans with beautiful burnished gold.
Chagall painted them hovering in the air,
And I paint them like my father and my mother.
The Jews are an eternal forest preserve
Where the trees stand dense, and even the dead
Cannot lie down. They stand upright, leaning on the living,
And you cannot tell them apart. Just that fire
Burns the dead faster.

And what about God? God lingered
Like the scent of a beautiful woman who once
Faced them in passing and they didn't see her face,
Only her fragrance remained, kinds of perfumes,
Blessed be the Creator of kinds of perfumes.

A Jewish man remembers the sukkah in his grandfather's home.
And the sukkah remembers for him
The wandering in the desert that remembers
The grace of youth and the Tablets of the Ten Commandments
And the gold of the Golden Calf and the thirst and the hunger
That remember Egypt.

And what about God? According to the settlement
Of divorce from the Garden of Eden and from the Temple,

God sees his children only once
A year, on Yom Kippur.

The Jews are not a historical people
And not even an archaeological people, the Jews
Are a geological people with rifts
And collapses and strata and fiery lava.
Their history must be measured
On a different scale.

The Jews are buffed by suffering and polished by torments
Like pebbles on the seashore.
The Jews are distinguished only in their death
As pebbles among other stones:
When the mighty hand flings them,
They skip two times, or three,
On the surface of the water before they drown.

Some time ago, I met a beautiful woman
Whose grandfather performed my circumcision
Long before she was born. I told her,
You don't know me and I don't know you
But we are the Jewish people,
Your dead grandfather and I the circumcised and you the beautiful grand-
    daughter
With golden hair: we are the Jewish people.

And what about God? Once we sang
*"There is no God like ours,"* now we sing, "There is no God of ours"
But we sing. We still sing.

The land knows where the clouds come from and whence the hot wind,
Whence hatred and whence love.
But its inhabitants are confused, their heart is in the East
And their body in the far West.*
Like migratory birds who lost their summer and winter,
Lost the beginning and the end, and they migrate
To the end of pain all their days.

The land can read and write,
Its eyes are open. It would be better
If it were ignorant as the people of the land,
Blind and groping
For its children without seeing them.

The Greater Land of Israel is like a fat and heavy woman,
And the State of Israel like a young woman,
Supple and thin-waisted,
But in both of them
Jerusalem is always the cunt of the land,
The unsated cunt,
The throbbing and screaming orgasm
Which won't end until Messiah comes.

*Line from a famous Zionist poem by Yehuda Halevi (1085–1140).

## ❧ TEMPORARY POEM ❧
## OF MY TIME

Hebrew writing and Arabic writing go from east to west,
Latin writing, from west to east.
Languages are like cats:
You must not stroke their hair the wrong way.
The clouds come from the sea, the hot wind from the desert,
The trees bend in the wind,
And stones fly from all four winds,
Into all four winds. They throw stones,
Throw this land, one at the other,
But the land always falls back to the land.
They throw the land, want to get rid of it,
Its stones, its soil, but you can't get rid of it.

They throw stones, throw stones at me
In 1936, 1938, 1948, 1988,
Semites throw at Semites and anti-Semites at anti-Semites,
Evil men throw and just men throw,
Sinners throw and tempters throw,
Geologists throw and theologists throw,
Archaeologists throw and archhooligans throw,
Kidneys throw stones and gall bladders throw,
Head stones and forehead stones and the heart of a stone,
Stones shaped like a screaming mouth
And stones fitting your eyes
Like a pair of glasses,
The past throws stones at the future,
And all of them fall on the present.
Weeping stones and laughing gravel stones,
Even God in the Bible threw stones,
Even the Urim and Tumim were thrown
And got stuck in the breastplate of justice,
And Herod threw stones and what came out was a Temple.

Oh, the poem of stone sadness
Oh, the poem thrown on the stones
Oh, the poem of thrown stones.
Is there in this land
A stone that was never thrown
And never built and never overturned
And never uncovered and never discovered
And never screamed from a wall and never discarded by the builders
And never closed on top of a grave and never lay under lovers
And never turned into a cornerstone?

Please do not throw any more stones,
You are moving the land,
The holy, whole, open land,
You are moving it to the sea
And the sea doesn't want it
The sea says, not in me.
Please throw little stones,
Throw snail fossils, throw gravel,
Justice or injustice from the quarries of Migdal Tsedek,
Throw soft stones, throw sweet clods,
Throw limestone, throw clay,
Throw sand of the seashore,
Throw dust of the desert, throw rust,
Throw soil, throw wind,
Throw air, throw nothing
Until your hands are weary
And the war is weary
And even peace will be weary and will be.

We did our duty.
We went out with our children
To gather mushrooms in the forest
Which we planted ourselves when we were children.

We learned the names of wildflowers
Whose aroma was
Like blood spilled in vain.
We laid a big love on small bodies,
We stood enlarged and shrunken in turn,
In the eyes of the holder of the binoculars,
Divine and mad.

And in the war of the sons of light and the sons of darkness
We loved the good and soothing darkness
And hated the painful light.
We did our duty,
We loved our children
More than our homeland,
We dug all the wells into the earth
And now we dig into the space of the skies,
Well after well, with no beginning, no end.

We did our duty,
The words *you shall remember* we changed to "we will forget"
As they change a bus schedule
When the direction of the route changes,
Or as they change the plaques
Of *Dew and Showers* and *He Who Brings Rain* in the synagogue
When the seasons change.

We did our duty,
We arranged our lives in flowerbeds and shadows
And straight paths, pleasant for walking,
Like the garden of a mental hospital.

Our despair is domesticated and gives us peace,
Only the hopes have remained,
Wild hopes, their screams
Shatter the night and rip up the day.

We did our duty.
We were like people entering a moviehouse,
Passing by those coming out, red-faced
Or pale, crying quietly or laughing aloud,
And they enter without a second glance, without
Turning back, into the light and the dark and the light.
We have done our duty.

## ➤ THIS IS THE LIFE ◄
## OF PROMISES

This is the life of promises. The Greek priest
Knows, the rabbi knows, the child at night knows,
My mother knew and died, the dead-may-God-revive-them know,
*The one in the fire and the one in the water,*
The one at his end and the one not at his end know
And are waiting together in the earth. Death promises
Revival, and life promises death. The false prophets
Prophesy infinite happiness,
The true prophets promise a bad and bitter end,
But a bad and bitter end is at least a sign
Of a good beginning and perhaps of a good and sweet middle.
For this is the life of promises,
Not a life of security. And this is not the promised land,
This is the land of promises.

The rosemary blooms in loving purple,
Dark orchards will produce shining fruit,
The beekeeper of Kfar Yonah in the Sharon Valley
Scatters his hives all over the country,
Even in the Negev Desert, to make honey without him,
And he goes round the country, checking from time to time.
A tire thrown into a wadi
Rests among the thorns like a martyred saint,
And the thorns wait for the softening springtime,
For this is the land of promises,
For this is the land of vows and oaths,
Their keeping and their breaking make its
Geography, tear up its valleys
And split its rifts, raise its hills,
Crush its craters so they won't find rest,
And make dry riverbeds and fill tributaries with water
To extinguish love and hate and to calm the sea.

And people in this land—some climb up
A high observation tower to see the places
They came from, and next to them people climb up to see
The places where they want to go,
And they speak to each other excitedly
With maps in their hands and point all around:
"We'll go there, yes, on that road" or "From there
We came, there we walked, there we stayed a day or two,
There we spent the night."
And some remain at the top of the tower
And won't come down. For this is the land of promises.
And hope and disappointment make holidays
And birth and death make celebrations,
And the land promises skies and the sky promises
God and God promises the land,
For this is the land of promises
And this is the city of promises.
And David's tomb is not his tomb
And Rachel's tomb is not her tomb
And the vows are not vows and the oaths are not oaths
And everything is masks and everything is masked with something else.
And beautiful women need to cover
Their holy places—
A flowery dress before love,
A striped dress after,
Many laces as of a tent in the desert,
Many straps as of a sail in the sea
(And there is no sea in Jerusalem), a loop for the night,
Hooks and snaps for the day. The soul is a zipper,
The soul is buttons. A golden tiara on the brow,
A broad belt around the waist, and a shining buckle
Is a crown of the lower kingdom
Promising higher love, for this is the city
Of promises.

In the narrow lanes near the Church of the Holy Sepulchre
I saw groups of Greeks, old men and women
Straying confused, like an ancient Greek chorus
That lost its tragedy.

470    *Yehuda Amichai*

I saw them wearing black,
Folded chairs gripped under their armpits
Like folded wings.

And most of them will be dead a year from now,
Like birds returning to their home from their home,
For this is the city of promises
And this is the land of promises
And this is the life of promises.

I saw in the street on a summer evening
I saw a woman writing words
On a paper spread on a locked wooden door,
She folded it and slipped it between the door and the doorpost
And went off.

I didn't see her face or the face of the man
Who will read the writing and not the words.

On my desk lies a rock with the inscription "Amen,"
Piece of a tombstone, remnant of a Jewish graveyard
Ruined a thousand years ago in the city of my birth.

One word, "Amen" carved deep in the stone,
Hard and final, Amen to all that was and will not return,
Soft Amen: chanting like a prayer,
Amen, Amen, may it be His will.

Tombstones crumble, words come and go, words are forgotten,
The lips that uttered them turned to dust,
Tongues die like people, other tongues come to life,
Gods in the sky change, gods come and go,
Prayers remain forever.

May 1994

# Index of First Lines

# Yehuda Amichai
## A Biographical Note

Yehuda Amichai was one of the first to use the spoken Israeli Hebrew language in poetry, with its directness and idiomatic ambiguities, along with many allusions and turns of phrase from the Bible and the Jewish prayer book. He was born in Würzburg, Germany, in 1924, and attended kindergarten and elementary school in the local Jewish school, where he learned German and Hebrew from the first grade on. In 1935 he immigrated to Israel with his family and has spent most of his life in Jerusalem. After graduation from a religious high school, he was drafted into the British army, where he served from 1942 to 1946. During the Israeli War of Independence (1948–49) he served in the Negev brigade of the Palmach. Amichai has published ten books of poetry, two novels, one volume of short stories, three children's books, and one volume of plays. His poetry has been translated into twenty-two languages, including Chinese and Japanese. He has participated in many poetry festivals and has received various prizes, including the Israel Prize in 1982. Amichai is married and has three children.